Scaasi

American Couturier

Pamela A. Parmal

with contributions by William DeGregorio

MFA Publications | Museum of Fine Arts, Boston

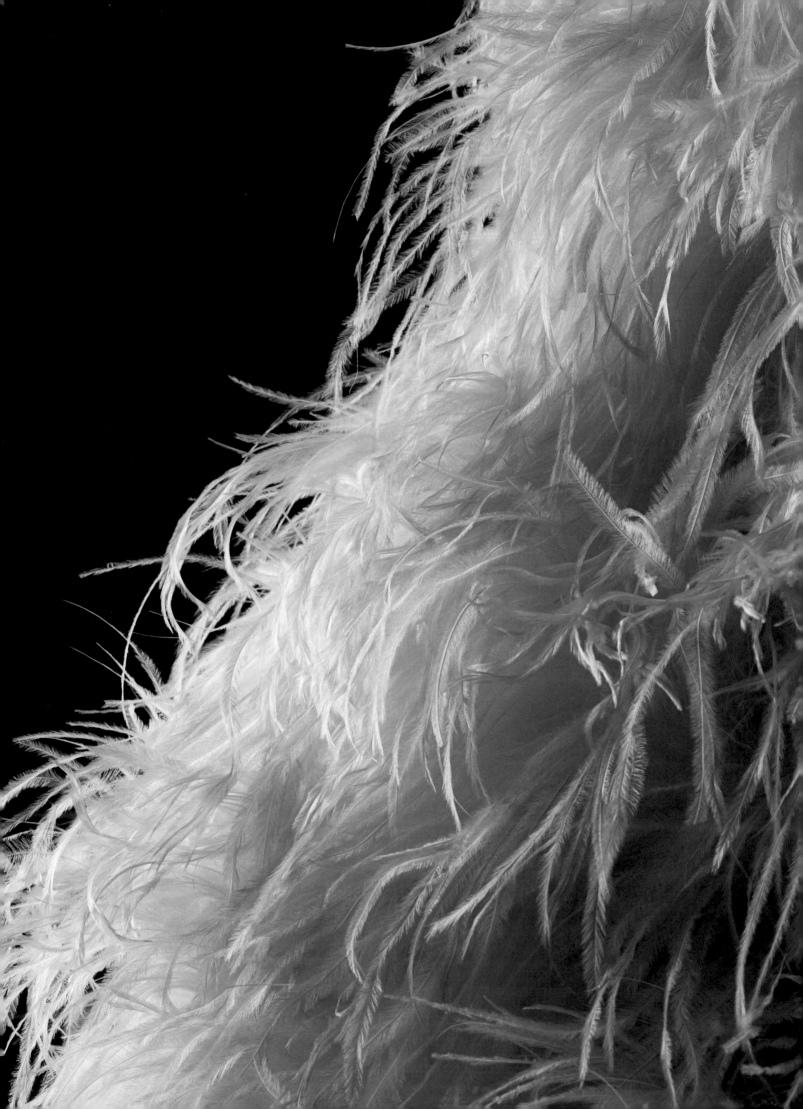

Contents

Director's Foreword

This book and the exhibition it accompanies celebrate the work of Arnold Scaasi. From the late 1950s and into the twenty-first century, Scaasi designed and made clothing for some of America's most famous and talented women. For much of his career he focused on custom design, creating a style that is luxurious, extravagant, and entirely his own. He also exercised firm control over his company and the world around him — so much so that his clients lovingly called him "He who must be obeyed." Fortunately, this attention to detail also extended to his record-keeping: Scaasi maintained an archive of drawings for almost every collection he made, along with patterns and press clippings that document his career from 1956 through 2009, the year his archive was acquired by the Museum of Fine Arts, Boston. Along with this acquisition, Scaasi graciously gave the Museum one hundred of his most important ensembles, for which we are deeply grateful.

Scaasi's archive was acquired thanks to the generosity of several Museum benefactors, including Jean S. and Frederic A. Sharf, Penny and Jeff Vinik, Lynne and Mark Rickabaugh, Jane and Robert Burke, Carol Wall, Mrs. I. W. Colburn, Megan O'Block, Lorraine Bressler, Daria Petrilli-Eckert, and anonymous donors. It is to Fred Sharf in particular that we are indebted for both the archive and the designer's gift of his garments. It was Fred who introduced Arnold to the MFA, and he used his considerable charm and enthusiasm to ensure that these important items found their way to Boston. His foresight, and his commitment to preserving not only art but also the history behind it, has helped the collections of the MFA grow and take new directions. The acquisition of Scaasi's archives and his donation of the outfits have allowed us to present a complete picture of the designer, showcasing the work and career of a true American couturier.

Finally, this book would not have been as beautiful and substantial a publication without the generosity of Ann and John Clarkeson and the fund they endowed, the Ann and John Clarkeson Lecture and Publication Fund for Textiles and Costumes. Their continued support of the David and Roberta Logie Department of Textile and Fashion Arts and the work of its staff is greatly appreciated.

Malcolm Rogers
Ann and Graham Gund Director
Museum of Fine Arts, Boston

Acknowledgments

The acquisition of the Arnold Scaasi collection and archive by the Museum of Fine Arts is a milestone in the Museum's collecting of twentieth-century fashion. The acquisition not only added more than 100 examples of the designer's work to our holdings, but has attracted other donations as well, including a group of twenty-three important dresses designed for Mrs. Saul Steinberg in the 1980s and 1990s, offered by Mrs. Steinberg. Even more transformative than the acquisition of the clothing has been the arrival of the designer's archive of sketches, press clippings, and patterns. With this material we can now better interpret Arnold Scaasi's achievements as a designer, his importance to twentieth-century fashion, and his working methods. The archive has been invaluable in writing this book and putting together the accompanying exhibition, and we can't thank Arnold Scaasi enough. Nor can we adequately thank the donors who made its acquisition possible: Jean S. and Frederic A. Sharf, Penny and Jeff Vinik, Lynne and Mark Rickabaugh, Jane and Robert Burke, Carol Wall, Mrs. I. W. Colburn, Megan O'Block, Lorraine Bressler, Daria Petrilli-Eckert, and anonymous donors.

Malcolm Rogers, Ann and Graham Gund Director, and Katherine Getchell, Deputy Director, provided support and guidance throughout this whole process; without them, the collection and archive would not be here. I would also like to give a special word of thanks to Museum trustee Frederic A. Sharf, who initiated this project and introduced Arnold Scaasi to the MFA. His dedication to the Museum, and his appreciation for art in all media and its history, have brought this remarkable collection to Boston and ensured that it remains available for generations to come. Fred Sharf's passion for presenting the facts has enriched the present book tremendously, and I am grateful to him for proofreading the text and for the hours he spent checking dates, interviewing Arnold Scaasi, and getting at the truth. His work has ensured that this book provides the most accurate information available in print.

The publication of a book is of course the work of many, and this one is no exception. My sincerest thanks go to everyone involved. William DeGregorio, Textile and Fashion Arts Department Assistant, used his formidable skills to locate and identify photographs, to research and write many of the captions, and to deal with the many organizational details involved in photographing and accessioning the archive. The rest of the department staff — Emily Banis, Alex Huff, Yvonne Markowitz, and Lauren Whitley — generously shared their expertise. The dazzling photographs of Scaasi's garments are the work of the MFA's Imaging Studios and of Michael Gould in particular, working closely in collaboration with the Textile

Conservation staff that so expertly dressed the garments: Claudia Iannuccilli, Masumi Kataoka, Meredith Montague, Allison Murphy, and Joel Thompson. Our publications department also deserves my sincere thanks for creating yet another beautiful book; I'm especially grateful to Mark Polizzotti for his skillful editing and to Terry McAweeney and Jodi Simpson for seeing the book through production. My thanks as well to Susan Marsh, who designed the publication with her usual refined sensibility.

Finally, my deepest thanks go to Arnold Scaasi, who had the wisdom to preserve his designs, patterns, and garments. We are very grateful that he chose the MFA as the home for his archive and had the confidence in our abilities to maintain and interpret his work for future audiences. I am also very grateful to his life partner, Parker Ladd, who has provided guidance and support along the way, as well as to Glendina Weste for assistance above and beyond the call.

Pamela A. Parmal
David and Roberta Logie Curator
of Textile and Fashion Arts

The Early Years

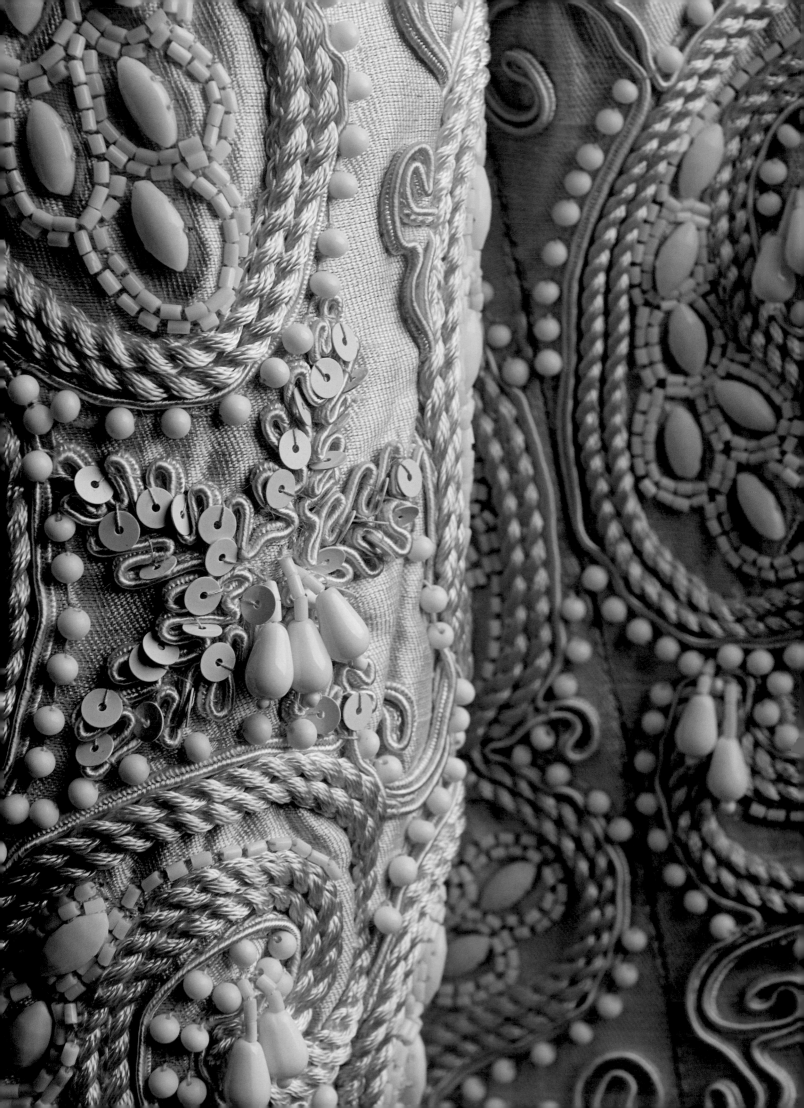

"When I was five or six, I remember *distinctly*, I vehemently told my mother she should not wear her corsage of gardenias on her shoulder, but that she should pin it to her evening bag. She happily complied, and I have been telling women what to wear and how to wear it ever since." So began, by his own recollection, the career of one of the most precocious, extravagant, yet refined designers in America.

Arnold Isaacs was born in Montreal on May 8, 1930, the son of a successful furrier. He demonstrated an interest in fashion at a young age, an interest that his family supported and that his female relatives in particular

Scaasi has said that his admiration for the fashions of the 1930s was influenced primarily by his Aunt Ida, shown here (center) with her husband, Samuel Wynn. "It was an era of fashion," Scaasi wrote in the October 29, 1962, issue of the *Philadelphia Inquirer*, "which . . . crystallized both femininity and simplicity for perhaps the first time since the medieval centuries," and it was an aesthetic from which he would draw inspiration throughout his career.

shared. Arnold's greatest inspiration, however, came from his Aunt Ida, whom he and his older sister Isobel went to stay with in Melbourne, Australia. Arnold remembers his aunt as being extremely stylish, wearing garments designed by the Parisian couturiers Elsa Schiaparelli, Madeleine Vionnet, and Coco Chanel. With Ida's encouragement, Arnold returned to Montreal after a year and began his studies at the Ecole Cotnoir-Capponi, the head of which had worked for years in the Paris couture industry. He remained with the school for a year and a half, studying draping, cutting patterns, and construction, and then moved to Paris to finish his training at the Ecole de la Chambre Syndicale de la Couture Parisienne. His education prepared him for a career that emphasized originality, classic design, and custom fitting — in contrast to the demands of the ready-to-wear industry in New York, where anonymous designers merely adapted the latest Paris fashions to suit the taste of American consumers.

Before leaving Paris for New York in 1952, Arnold worked for about two months at the couture house of Paquin — an apprenticeship that further emphasized originality and high style and gave him good training in how to run a custom-design business for a select clientele. In New York, he soon found work assisting Charles James, one of the few custom designers still working in the city, and perhaps the best to appreciate the couture skills Arnold had learned in Paris. James was widely known for the extraordinarily sculptural and luxurious clothing he designed for some of America's most sophisticated women. Unfortunately, James was also known for his mercurial nature and lack of business sense: Arnold's apprenticeship not only exposed him to extraordinary clothing, but also showed him how *not* to treat important clients and run a business.

After working with James, Arnold designed for a number of manufacturers on Seventh Avenue, in the process forming connections within the industry and creating a name for himself. During this period, he worked for Pauline Trigère and the ready-to-wear manufacturer Samuel

Winston (for whom Charles James also created designs), and made runway garments for the milliners Lilly Daché and Mr. Fred in his spare time. By 1954, while maintaining his Seventh Avenue commitments, Arnold had established a small custom-design business in his second-floor walk-up apartment on East Fifty-eighth Street and hired a seamstress and a tailor to help him. Through previous contacts and word of mouth, he built up a small but select clientele that included such stylish women as Irma Schlesinger, mother of the prominent socialite Nan Kempner; Mary Tae Nichols, wife of the editor of the *New York Times Magazine*; the fashion model Gillis McGill, whom he had met when designing for Lilly Daché; and the stage and television star Arlene Francis. As these women began wearing his designs, word of his unique and finely crafted clothes quickly spread. With the help and support of several women involved in the fashion press and public relations, including Bettina Ballard, Muriel Maxwell, and Jane Gray, Arnold extended his business into what proved to be a lucrative sideline: custom-designing clothes for advertisements, including spreads for Scott tissue, Monsanto, and the 1954 "Body by Fisher" campaign for General Motors — which also saw the first use of his trademark name.

In 1955, Arnold Isaacs, now known to the fashion world as Arnold Scaasi, was asked to create a line of coats and dresses for the manufacturer Dressmaker Casuals. At the time, it was customary for designers of such garments to remain anonymous, but Scaasi's name appeared in advertisements and promotions for the new line. The collection was shown in May and garnered very positive press. Arnold designed for the company for another year, before launching his own ready-to-wear collection in 1956. It can't have hurt that the cover of *Vogue*'s December 1955 issue featured a Scaasi design: a red satin evening coat from his spring Dressmaker Casuals line. The groundwork for Arnold Scaasi's future success had been set, and he exploded onto the American fashion scene.

Gillis McGill was a successful runway model before becoming Scaasi's muse and the model he used to fit his dresses, starting in 1955. When McGill debuted the designer's green feather dress (see p. 46) at the Bachelor's Ball in New York City, Babe Paley reportedly called it the most beautiful dress she had ever seen.

Opposite:
With its "stiff, beautiful, Kabuki-like folds," Arnold's opera coat of vermillion satin made an architectural statement on the cover of *Vogue*'s Christmas issue of 1955. Credited solely to Arnold Scaasi, the coat retailed for $235.

VOGUE

DECEMBER

opposite page 16

CHRISTMAS ISSUE

...pages to treasure

50 CENTS

Couture and Custom Design

The haute couture system in which Arnold Scaasi was trained developed in Paris during the second half of the nineteenth century. The designer, or couturier, would prepare two collections a year, each composed of a series of garments, or models, that were shown to clients on dress forms or on live mannequins. A client could choose the model she preferred and the couture house would make up the garment to her exact measurements. The contemporary Paris couture system works in a similar fashion, with new collections introduced in spring and fall at lavish fashion shows. In the couture houses, the couturier reigns supreme, although models are often adjusted to suit the taste and figure of the client. In dressmaking, by contrast, the client provides the fabric and works more collaboratively with the dressmaker to decide on the style of the garment.

Arnold's training at the Chambre Syndicale school in Paris introduced him to the world of French couture and emphasized three goals in particular: knowledge of the garment based on the criteria of quality and fit, development of creative flair, and knowledge of the professional environment. Arnold brought these principles with him to New York, and throughout his career he has held to them and to the high standards of his training. Even his ready-to-wear collections are renowned for the custom look he was able to give them.

Four-and-a-half yards of Bianchini silk brocade and subtle draping ensured a voluminous shape for this opera coat, which appeared in the October 1958 issue of *Harper's Bazaar.* The bell-shaped silhouette, short sleeves, and portrait neckline are all signature Scaasi design elements.

The pattern on this coat has been matched across the long vertical front seam, creating geometric unity. The handmade buttonholes give the coat a custom look.

Opposite:
Scaasi's sketches for this ensemble depict a voluminous strapless dress with an asymmetrical gathered bodice. At least one version of it, however, has thin straps and a much simpler bodice, modifications probably made for a specific client. The inventory of materials used for the coat lists the price and quantity for each, as well as the final wholesale price of $225.

A slight social faux pas allows us to see, side-by-side, two variations on a single theme. Here, Sally Kirkland of *Life* and Mary Jane Pool of *Vogue* discuss their respective Scaasi designs at the Coty American Fashion Critics' Awards, held at the Metropolitan Museum of Art in 1960.

This coat and dress, fashioned from the same Ottoman-inspired silk as Kirkland's and Pool's ensembles, was featured in an ad for Woodward & Lothrop, a large department store located in Washington, D.C., that continued to retail Arnold's more lavish designs throughout the 1960s. The sketch shows Scaasi's original design for the dress.

The many versions of this dress and coat ensemble that appear in the designer's press clippings from 1960 attest to his ability to adapt and reimagine his designs while keeping his favored fabric choice constant. Scaasi called this color "golden peach."

Charles James

Arnold arrived in New York with the specific aim of working for the American designer Charles James. He later recalled approaching Christian Dior for a job while still in Paris and, when he mentioned that he had an introduction to James, being told by Dior: "Charles James is the greatest dressmaker in America, and if you have even a chance to work with him, it's madness to stay in Paris and work for nothing as an apprentice. Go do it."

During the period that Arnold stayed with James, he soaked up everything the designer could teach him. James was famous for his elaborate evening dresses made of contrasting silk fabrics in jewel-toned colors. Unlike most designers, who created garments by draping cloth over a mannequin and letting the human form give it shape, he often treated his garments as sculptures, building complex structures underneath the cloth, at times with twenty-five or thirty sections, to help the clothes maintain their form. Some of these structures were so stiff that women could not sit down in the dresses and had to carry their clothes to gala events, only putting them on once they had arrived. Despite such inconveniences, James's dresses were worn by the best-dressed women of the time, including Austine Hearst, Millicent Rogers, and Dominique de Menil. Several of James's clients later became Arnold's clients.

Arnold and James understood one another; they certainly shared a similar approach to design, as well as an appreciation for their clients and their extravagant lifestyles. Arnold, like James, has

In May 1964, Austine Hearst was among the many starlets and socialites who attended Scaasi's first couture collection. She later became Scaasi's client, ordering from his fall 1982 collection this blue tiered gown with coordinating shawl in which Scaasi adapted James's construction techniques to create a dress of dramatic sculptural appeal.

The understructure for this gown consists of two inner petticoats stiffened with horsehair and multiple layers of tulle in different shades of blue that would be just visible as the wearer walked.

become known for his elaborate evening wear, adapting James's technique of building understructures for his evening and cocktail dresses, which are often fitted with a boned bodice and have bouffant underskirts created with yards of tulle ruffles. Arnold is one of the few designers to learn these techniques from James. Soon after leaving James's employ, he designed coats for Dressmaker Casuals that were built on a canvas foundation to give them a structured look. Unlike James, however, whose work often resembled architecture, Arnold created a light structure that made for a softer, more fluid garment.

The two men also differed in their business practices. James was known to make a client wait two years for a gown, not willing to relinquish it until he considered it perfect. "I am not a designer," he once said; "designers are hired help that only copy what's in the wind. They don't create fashion. Only a couturier does this, with his client as inspiration." Arnold, though also exacting in his standards, learned early on the importance of keeping his customers satisfied, and throughout his career built a loyal and steadfast clientele.

Above:
The renowned photographer Cecil Beaton was a close friend of James, and promoted his work early on in the pages of *Vogue*. This shot, from the May 10, 1930, issue, features James's friend Tilly Losch in a cloche-like turban for his label Boucheron.

Left:
James's flair for the dramatic certainly rubbed off on Scaasi, who created this striking polka-dot ensemble in 1959. It was photographed on model Sunny Harnett on the runway of Newark Airport for *Life*.

Opposite:
James's "Butterfly" gown from 1954 is one of his most famous and extravagant creations. Worn by Austine Hearst and here modeled by Gypsy Rose Lee, it was featured in ads for Du Pont nylon, a campaign in which Scaasi also took part.

By using concentric layers of tulle in various colors, James gave the dress a changeable quality that made it appear as gossamer-like as the wings of a butterfly. The inner structure, only hinted at here, consists of a much more rigid system of supports that made the gown quite cumbersome, though photogenic.

"Body by Fisher"

Arnold's custom-design clients included not only fashionable women and celebrities, but commercial entities as well — most notably advertising firms. One of his first jobs was for the 1954 "Body by Fisher" campaign, which Kudner Associates developed for General Motors. The agency hired the prominent photographer Edgar de Evia to photograph the luxury cars in sophisticated locations, flanked by famous fashion models in clothing designed by French couturiers and New York designers. De Evia's life partner at the time, Robert Denning, was an interior designer who had changed his name to fit his lifestyle; Denning suggested

Scaasi literally made a name for himself with the 1954 "Body by Fisher" campaign for GM, which featured this red dress and matching coat. The campaign, one of the biggest and most successful of the 1950s, ran well into the next decade.

The design of this dress proved so successful that Scaasi reintroduced it for his fall 1958 collection, and incorporated certain elements of its design throughout his career. In 1984, he created a version for Diahann Carroll to wear to the Golden Globe awards (see p. 107).

Opposite:
Called "Scaasi's felt fantasy," this yellow maternity dress with deep pleats was actually used to illustrate an ad for Mennen Baby Magic oil in 1959.

Bottom left:
In 1959, the Scott company charged various designers, including Count Sarmi and Sybil Connolly, to design dresses to match their pastel-tinted bathroom tissue. Scaasi designed many lavish gowns, such as this one in pink chiffon, another in pleated yellow chiffon, and an over-the-top white *point d'esprit* example.

Bottom right:
Although most of the ads in which Scaasi's designs appear feature his highly photogenic evening wear, this ad makes use of the designer's sportier looks to emphasize playfulness and youth.

that Arnold, who was still using his birth name at this point, do likewise — and thus Arnold Isaacs became Arnold Scaasi. The more Italian-sounding name was better suited to the fashion world at a time when Italian designers like Pucci, Sorelle Fontana, and Galitzine were easily recognized.

De Evia was known for his softly focused, often diffused images. Arnold's luxurious evening dress and coat of red and orange satin contrasted beautifully with the soft pink tones of the convertible against which it was photographed. The ensemble caught the notice of many, including former fashion editors Muriel Maxwell and Jane Gray, who had recently formed a public-relations firm. They sought out the young designer and hired him to create clothing for a Lucky Strike ad. The long and fruitful relationship that ensued saw the two women progress from being Arnold's clients to being his friends and publicity agents.

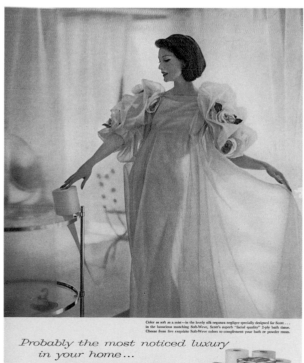

Color as soft as a mist—in the lovely silk organza negligee specially designed for Scott . . . in the luxurious matching Soft-Weve, Scott's superb "facial quality" 2-ply bath tissue. Choose from five exquisite Soft-Weve colors to complement your bath or powder room.

*Probably the most noticed luxury
in your home . . .*

Soft-Weve by **Scott**

The car that's all the things you are . . .
THE NEW FORD THUNDERBIRD

It's you stepping out—
Your new Thunderbird might have been specially designed for gala evenings; it has a flair and distinctive elegance all its own. And its doors are so wide you can sweep in and out with bouffant gown unruffled—and your poise intact!

It's you in your play mood—
Smart, original, versatile . . . your new Thunderbird is in the mood for fun when you are. This car is always *fun* to drive because, bless its heart, *it's just your size!* It's roomy yet compact, a joy to handle . . . and so easy to park!

It's you, the Leader—
You set the style, you set the pace wherever you go, driving the prestige car every woman would love to own. Yet the 1959 Thunderbird actually costs *far less* than other luxury cars. See your Ford dealer. Drive this jewel of a car!

America's most becoming car!

Arlene Francis

The Broadway actress and television star Arlene Francis met Scaasi shortly after he started his custom-design business in 1954. They were introduced by Muriel Maxwell and Jane Gray, who brought the star to Scaasi's East Fifty-eighth Street walk-up. Over the years, Arnold would create costumes for Francis's roles on the Broadway stage and her wardrobes for the TV game show *What's My Line?* and *Home*, the afternoon show she hosted. *Home*, which premiered on NBC in 1954 as part of a trilogy of news programs that included *Today* and *Tonight*, was the network's first attempt to develop a show directed primarily at a female audience. One of the more outlandish outfits Scaasi designed for Francis, which she wore when she guest-hosted *The Jack Paar Show* in July 1962, featured a pair of ice blue wool chaps trimmed with fox fur: they generated a great deal of comment in the press. Arnold's work for Francis and for other TV, concert, and Broadway stars, such as Eva Gabor, Lauren Bacall, and Joan Sutherland, quickly taught him how to please his celebrity clients and how to make them look good on the stage or the small screen.

Playwright Harold Kurnitz, on seeing the ensemble Scaasi created for Francis to wear in the climactic scene in *Once More, with Feeling*, added an exchange between Francis and Joseph Cotten, who played her egomaniacal conductor husband. When Cotten compliments his wife on her attire, she replies, "Oh this old thing? I picked it up in Macy's basement years ago." She then throws open the coat to reveal the silver dress with matching coat lining, thrilling the audience.

Francis was initially apprehensive of Scaasi's plan to include an otter fur coat in the costumes for *Once More, with Feeling* because of her character's profession, a teacher. Undaunted, Scaasi convinced Francis and Kurnitz that the luxurious garments were entirely appropriate.

In the play *Once More, with Feeling*, which opened in October 1958, Francis played a plain-Jane music teacher married to a cele-brated composer/conductor. The initial thought was to dress her in humble garments; Arnold saw things differently, however, and encouraged Francis to wear glamorous clothes suitable for the wife of a famous conductor. He designed a coat of sheared otter fur with Norwegian blue fox collar and lining for her grand entrance on stage. For the final scene, Francis wore an evening ensemble with a coat of red satin that opened to reveal a silver lamé lining and a dress of the same fabric. The use of matching fabric for both dress and coat lining became a signature Scaasi design element.

In 1954, Francis appeared on the cover of *Newsweek*, alongside Eleanor Roosevelt and First Lady Mamie Eisenhower (another Scaasi client), as one of the three "most popular women in America." Photo-graphed here on the set of the *Home* show, Francis, with her unique, plummy delivery and refined Scaasi wardrobe, became an icon of the new tele-vision medium.

For his 1962 resort collection, Scaasi designed this suit with a long coat encrusted with beads and braids in a paisley pattern. It was later worn by Francis on the Valentine's Day 1965 episode of *What's My Line?*

Dressmaker Casuals

The New York ready-to-wear industry of the mid-twentieth century divided itself into two main groups: the coat and suit manufacturers and the dress manufacturers. This distinction paralleled the workrooms of the Paris couture houses, which were divided between the *tailleur* (literally, "tailored") and the *flou* (hazy, soft): that is, between the tailoring workroom that specialized in coats and suits and the one that focused on soft construction characteristic of dresses. Despite its name, Dressmaker Casuals focused on making coats and suits, and in 1955 the company hired Arnold Scaasi to be its in-house designer. Previously, Charles James had worked for the company in the same role, an indication of its interest in progressive design. Contrary to Seventh Avenue practice at the time, which held that in-house designers remain anonymous, Scaasi insisted that his name be associated with the label.

Arnold's first collection for Dressmaker Casuals debuted in May 1955 to critical acclaim and made his name a household word. The *Milwaukee Journal* (July 1955) described the collection as "highly imaginative," and Arnold was proclaimed "a rising star on the fashion horizon" by the *Philadelphia Inquirer Magazine* on August 28. Many fashion writers remarked that the collection had a custom-made look to it — another rarity for Seventh Avenue. One reporter noted the link between Scaasi's collection, with its use of imaginative bombée and split-level shapes, and the work of Charles James.

Scaasi's work for Dressmaker Casuals made him a celebrity at the young age of twenty-five. He continued designing for the company until May 1956, when he launched a ready-to-wear line of his own.

This image, shot in the Metropolitan Museum of Art, appeared in the November 1955 *Vogue*. The coat on the left, eucalyptus green satin with a brown velvet lining, is from Dressmaker Casuals. Both hats in the picture are by Lilly Daché, for whom Arnold worked in the early 1950s.

Scaasi's first collection for Dressmaker Casuals led the *Philadelphia Inquirer Magazine* (August 1955) to proclaim, "A STAR is born!"

Dressmaker Casuals, Inc.

wish to announce
the showing of their

FALL COLLECTION

COATS • SUITS • COSTUMES

by SCAASI

commencing
Thursday May 19 at 10:30 a.m. *(invitation only)*
Thereafter daily at 2 p.m.

512 Seventh Avenue N.Y. 18

LAckawanna 4-4764

This photo of a Dress-maker Casuals suit by Scaasi ran in the April 3, 1956, issue of *Look* under the headline "The Girl in the Gray Flannel Suit," a play on the recent film *The Man in the Gray Flannel Suit* starring Gregory Peck and Jennifer Jones.

Scaasi's designs for Dressmaker Casuals are among the most experimental he ever produced. The red coat on the left, known as "Bombée," was heavily photographed by the press and described by *Women's Wear Daily* on May 20, 1955, as heralding the new "almond line."

"I love Seventh Avenue," Scaasi told the *New York Journal American* in 1955, when he was working on the fabled avenue of clothing manufacturers, at number 512. On September 20, 1955, *Women's Wear Daily* proclaimed this display for Russek's in New York their "Window of the Week."

Against a ruby-red background and carpet with glittering crystal columns, nine mannequins were dressed in Scaasi's fall line and one-of-a-kind hats he had designed especially for this presentation.

The Scaasi Label

The first Scaasi ready-to-wear collection debuted in May 1956, launched at the urging of buyers from several major department stores, including Henri Bendel, Neiman Marcus, and I. Magnin. Arnold designed and produced the twenty-three dresses — as he did all his custom clothing — in his small apartment on East Fifty-eighth Street. The collection was presented at the Plaza Hotel and became an immediate success with the press and department-store buyers. *Women's Wear Daily* for May 29 cited the designer's architectural approach, which allowed for clothing with uncluttered lines and intricate construction. The paper singled out the evening gowns as "truly spectacular" and remarked on the "big impression" made by the unusual colors.

Opposite:
This bubble-skirted dress (center) show-cases Scaasi's ability to display his fabric choice to maximum effect while still employing intricate draping and pleating. The same model was worn by both Patrice Munsel and Arlene Francis, and is shown here, among garments by other designers, in the December 1960 issue of *Life*, as part of a retrospective of the previous twenty-five years in fashion.

Scaasi puts the finishing touches to model Gillis McGill for the showing of his first ready-to-wear collection at the Plaza Hotel on May 28, 1956. McGill and Scaasi first met when she modeled for Lilly Daché. Arnold designed the clothing to be worn with Daché's hats in her 1954 shows.

While buyers throughout the United States picked up the collection, Arnold didn't leave its promotion to the stores. Indefatigably, he traveled across the country, bringing his work to his customers. Arnold continued to show his work this way into the 1990s, which allowed him both to introduce his complete line to the public (rather than just the models purchased by the stores) and to gauge current tastes and preferences through direct contact with consumers. The increased exposure made the Scaasi name recognizable all over America. According to *Time* magazine, by the end of 1962 Arnold employed a studio staff of thirty-five, launched two hundred new models a year, and sold to seventy-five different stores. He also began licensing arrangements and created collections of men's sweaters and ties, children's clothing, jewelry, and handbags.

By the end of 1958, Scaasi designs had twice graced the covers of both *Harper's Bazaar* and *Vogue*; his collection had been shown in Washington with other American designers at the request of Mamie Eisenhower; and he had designed costumes for Arlene Francis (in *Once More, with Feeling*), Eva Gabor (in the Noël Coward play *Present Laughter*), and the opera singer Patrice Munsel. His success enabled him to buy a Stanford White town house on West Fifty-sixth Street, setting up business on the lower three floors and living on the top two. That same year ended with Scaasi's winning the coveted "Winnie" — the Coty American Fashion Critics' Award for designer of the year. Though not yet thirty, his hard work, talent, and drive had already brought him to the top of the fashion industry.

Scaasi's workroom could be found on the third floor of the West Fifty-sixth Street town house. An article in Toronto's *Star Weekly* on June 18, 1960, featured photos of the designer at work. Like a French couturier, Arnold often built his clothing on a live model.

Opposite:
The June 10, 1959, edition of the *New York Times* featured an article on Scaasi and his quick rise to fame. The article included pictures of Scaasi's new town house and an image of the designer behind his antique desk.

By the early 1960s, Scaasi began his move towards couture by using extremely expensive specialty fabrics, such as those in this series of jackets in 1961. The flowers were handmade in France especially for Scaasi, and the jackets cost $200, or about $1,400 today.

Peter Fink photographed Arnold's spring 1960 collection in the West Fifty-sixth Street town house. Sunny Harnett, a top model at the time and one of Scaasi's favorites, was posed in an extravagant pink gown with purple evening coat against the Pompeian red doors, next to one of the two large black figures that welcomed guests to the salon. On the right, she wears the designer's green degradé ostrich dress with matching coat. Arnold also created a version in shades of orange and red with a pink velvet coat for Lauren Bacall to wear in the play *Goodbye Charlie* on Broadway.

Arnold fully embraced patterned fabrics, often bold and unusual. For his spring and fall 1961 collections, he collaborated with the venerable British firm Liberty & Co., which had recently released a series of limited-edition prints called the Lotus Collection, inspired by Art Nouveau designs. Arnold used the Eustacia pattern on this dress and shawl and cut the bodice asymmetrically to conform to the pattern. His "free form" and "metronome" silhouettes are shown in sketches.

Diana Vreeland

The legendary fashion editor Diana Vreeland gave her encouragement to Scaasi shortly after he showed his first ready-to-wear collection at the Plaza Hotel in 1956. "Your clothes are perfectly beautiful," she exclaimed in a letter of February 16, "the colors and fabrics are divine." In June 1958, after Arnold designed his first fur collection for Ben Kahn, Vreeland sent further encouragement in the form of a telegram: "THANK YOU FOR THE WONDERFUL TREAT YOU HAVE COMBINED SPLENDOUR AND TASTE STOP JEWELRY FABRIC EVERYTHING SUPERB." But perhaps the greatest encouragement of all was that *Harper's Bazaar*, where Vreeland had worked since 1936, featured Scaasi designs in at least four editorial shoots between 1955 and 1958 and on the covers of the March, August, and September 1958 issues. The March and September issues, the two most important of the year, previewed the New York and Paris spring and fall collections.

"Elegance is good taste plus a dash of daring." This was *Harper's Bazaar* editor Carmel Snow's motto, but it could easily have been Scaasi's as well. From 1934 to 1958, Snow (left), along with her fashion editor Diana Vreeland (right), who remained with the magazine until 1971, dictated elegance from the pages of *Bazaar*, often discovering new talents, like Scaasi, along the way.

The red, white, and blue palette of this September 1958 cover was meant to symbolically convey the link between the latest Paris collections and those shown in the United States. According to Arnold, Vreeland so wanted to feature this coat on the cover that she implored him to find an alternative blue wool fabric made by an American manufacturer instead of the original textile from the French firm Rodier.

Scaasi's collaboration with furrier Ben Kahn garnered abundant attention from the press, including Vreeland, who sent this flattering telegram after witnessing the designer's first collection for Kahn in 1958. Here a male model and Sunny Harnett wear coats of Russian timber wolf lined in blue felt.

Scaasi found inspiration in butterflies for his spring 1958 collection. He used fabrics patterned with the insects and designed jewelry to coordinate, including butterfly headdresses like the one depicted in this *Chicago Daily Tribune* illustration from July 7, 1958. Scaasi called this dramatic silhouette the "bellows jumper."

This illustration, drawn by a young Andy Warhol for the *New York Times* in August 1961, shows a rectangular brooch from Arnold at its center. Jewelry continues to be an important part of the Scaasi empire to this day.

In 2008, when he began selling jewelry for the Home Shopping Network on cable television, Scaasi credited Vreeland for encouraging him to design his own jewelry line, which he'd first introduced in his fall 1958 collection. The collection was inspired by the shape and color of butterflies. Dresses with names like "Grand Papillon" were fashioned out of fabrics patterned with the diaphanous insects in black on red silk or in green cut velvet. Collars extended over the shoulders with dramatic flourish, suggesting butterfly wings. Pursuing this theme, the jewelry included rhinestone butterflies that appeared in necklaces and as hair ornaments or pins. Arnold designed jewelry until 1962, when he concluded that the collection involved too much work for too little financial return.

Scaasi began dressing actress, television personality, and philanthropist Kitty Carlisle Hart in 1958, when he made her a draped white chiffon strapless gown for the London premiere of *My Fair Lady*. Over the simple dress, he draped a startling evening coat of light blue moiré shot with silver threads and lined with white fox. Here Hart wears one of Scaasi's coat and cocktail dress ensembles in a cut-velvet butterfly pattern from the spring 1958 collection.

Scaasi's lavish designs and draping impressed many fashion editors during the late 1950s. This white *point d'esprit* evening dress from his fall/winter 1958 collection was featured in several newspaper stories and an ad for Revlon. Note the butterfly headdress worn with the diaphanous dress.

Mamie Eisenhower

This red coat from Scaasi's fall 1959 collection was one of the first pieces Mamie Eisenhower bought from the designer, and it quickly became a favorite. She was often photographed wearing it along with a matching red cap and gloves. The color became known as "Mamie red."

In October 1958, Scaasi was invited to Washington, D.C., to participate in an international fashion summit at the American Newspaper Women's Club, along with Pierre Balmain of Paris and Mikol Fontana of Rome. Following a morning press conference, the designers were taken to the White House to meet President Eisenhower and enjoy tea with the First Lady. Mamie Eisenhower was a fan of fashionable and beautiful clothing, and her wardrobe choices were widely reported in the press. Evidently she appreciated Arnold's luxurious style and taste: she ordered several ensembles from him for her fall 1959 wardrobe and continued to wear his clothes for the rest of her life.

Before Mrs. Eisenhower's wardrobe could be made, the new client had to be measured and the numbers recorded. Arnold felt that the sixty-five measurements he habitually took — more than are normally taken by French couturiers and dressmakers — were necessary not only to understand the client's proportions but also to understand her posture and how she moved. The measurements could then be used to prepare a dress form so the clothing could be correctly sized in the workroom. To ensure the proper fit, Arnold would travel to the White House and work with Mrs. Eisenhower personally.

The relationship between client and designer is an intimate one, and Mrs. Eisenhower worked closely with Arnold to select gowns that would be appropriate for the coming season. One of the most renowned dresses was a gold damask evening gown that the First Lady wore to a state dinner in honor of Soviet premier Nikita Khrushchev and his wife on September 15, 1959. According to Arnold, it was he who recommended that gold damask be worn for the affair, as a symbol of the United States' newfound wealth and position of power. Mrs. Eisenhower not only took his advice but also had the dinner coordinated with the garment: food was served in the gold-draped State Dining Room and gold-colored flowers decorated the tables.

President and Mrs. Eisenhower stand next to Premier and Mrs. Nikita Khrushchev during the state dinner held in the Khrushchevs' honor on September 15, 1959. Mamie wears a gold damask dress that Arnold made specifically for the occasion. The sketch for the dress illustrates the dramatic bustle effect of the back.

Opposite:
In the fall of 1959, Mrs. Eisenhower ordered several evening dresses from Scaasi, including this strapless rose-colored chiné taffeta, shown in a short cocktail version in his collection. The dramatically pleated back skirt shows a similar construction to the gold dress worn for the Khrushchev state dinner.

Mamie Eisenhower ordered six ensembles from Scaasi's spring 1960 collection, often wearing the evening dresses at White House events. The floral gown with a ruffled hem was made full length for Mrs. Eisenhower to wear to the state dinner for the king and queen of Thailand during a visit in July 1960. The strapless white chiffon gown with green accent was worn while entertaining the king and queen of Nepal that same year.

839

Fall 1961

Arnold presented his fall 1961 collection in his new showrooms at 550 Seventh Avenue, which, like his town house on West Fifty-sixth Street, were decorated by Valerian Rybar. Arnold had decided to move his business from the town house because, as he put it in the book *Scaasi: A Cut Above*, he felt like a prisoner of the building: living on the top floors and spending most of his time working on the lower ones, it was as if he never went out! The show was scheduled after 5 p.m., and as usual he requested that guests wear black tie. Violins played and the champagne flowed.

Reviewing the show, *Women's Wear Daily* wrote: "Every Scaasi collection is like a superb fabric documentary." From the very beginning of his career, Arnold's collections have evolved from the fabric. Before he even began to design a collection, Arnold selected his fabrics, traveling to Europe to find the most unique and luxurious textiles. He then arranged them in color groups, which would form the basic sequences of his runway shows. Once the fabrics were in hand, he would work with them, draping the cloth and allowing it to lead the way to the final garment. This focus on the presentation of the collection from the very beginning of the design process gave his runway shows pacing and variety.

One of the most-photographed looks in Scaasi's fall 1961 collection was a chinchilla-lined coat ensemble. As the model walked down the runway, she took off the coat to reveal a matching tweed skirt; the skirt was then removed to uncover a gray chiffon two-piece dress. As one reviewer noted, the ensemble was ideal for travel.

This coat in robin's-egg wool fleece features pockets that are cut on a curved seam, a technique Scaasi might have adapted from the French couture.

When Scaasi first learned he would be dressing Joan Crawford for this *Holiday* magazine spread, he was apprehensive about meeting the famously icy star — and his concern only grew when the actress greeted him in a plain white robe and no makeup. Scaasi feared she would appear foolishly over the hill in his sexy "Blue Meteor" gown and coat of billowing blue tulle; but Crawford, the consummate movie star, transformed herself for the occasion into a striking figure of poise and elegance.

Scaasi termed his finale gowns for the collection the "Evening Galaxy" sequence. Crawford opted for the blue version of this sheath, but there was also a red version (appropriately called "Red Meteor"), priced at $2,000 (roughly $14,000 today), and a nude version called "Morning Star."

   Unlike the French couture shows — which invariably began with day wear; segued into cocktail, dinner, and evening dresses; and finished with the wedding dress — Arnold often began his shows with evening wear to make a dramatic statement from the start. At times he mixed day and cocktail wear in what he called his "color stories," creating variety and drama. Always, however, he finished his shows with elaborate evening dresses, and the fall 1961 collection was no different. The final sequence of the show was titled "Evening Galaxy" and included dresses called "North Star," "Evening Star," "Shooting Star," and "Morning Star," ending with sequined sheathed gowns with tulle coats titled "Blue Meteor" and "Red Meteor," which had the audience roaring with approval.

These sketches are shown in the order in which Arnold presented the garments on the runway, illustrating his carefully constructed "color stories" — groups of ensembles with similar chromatic palates — and thematic variations. The short ombré cocktail dresses, made by hand-layering different colored chiffons, were called "Flash! Flash!" and appear with differing bodices, skirts, and sleeves to appeal to a variety of clients

  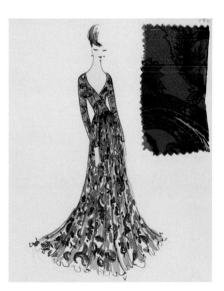

Taking inspiration from the American designer Gilbert Adrian's most luxurious and ambitious Hollywood costume commission up until that point, *Camille* (1936) starring Greta Garbo, Scaasi created his "Shooting Star" evening gown from ninety-five yards of white tulle with gold and silver embroidery.

Scaasi carried over a few Liberty & Co. prints from spring 1961 into his fall collection, using their paisleys in a variety of color schemes, including this wool coat and matching chiffon dress captured by *Vogue* on Cyd Charisse. Trimmed with black fisher (a fur of Canadian origin), the ensemble was lauded in the press as "truly devastating" and was naturally accessorized with Scaasi earrings.

Dina Merrill, the beautiful daughter of cereal heiress Marjorie Merriweather Post, became a loyal client of Scaasi in the early 1960s, while she was married to Stanley M. Rumbough, Jr. Here, she models Scaasi's "Twilight Zinnia" ensemble of a long dress under a short wrap trimmed with white marabou. The *New York Herald Tribune* noted that the effect of the fabric was of "flowers strewn like jewels across cut-velvet."

"I don't believe in making little nothings," Scaasi told *Holiday,* and his "Coat of Mail," embroidered with silvery-black square paillettes, is emblematic of his more daring design aesthetic. Although it may appear cumbersome, it was apparently quite lightweight and reportedly uncrushable.

Serena Russell Balfour

In 1962, Serena Russell, the daughter of Lady Sarah Spencer Churchill and granddaughter of Consuelo Vanderbilt, Duchess of Marlborough, celebrated her coming out at her ancestral home, Blenheim Palace in Oxfordshire, during the twenty-first birthday celebration for her cousin Lord Charles Spencer Churchill. Lady Sarah, a client of Scaasi now living in New York, asked that he design her and her daughter's wardrobes for the event. One of the biggest commissions of Arnold's career, it introduced his name to members of high society in the United States and Europe.

For Russell, Arnold designed a debutante dress of white covered with appliquéd flowers, a white fitted silk-and-wool coat, and a dress of navy and white polka dots to be worn at Ascot when she met Queen Elizabeth, and ensembles to be worn for luncheons, tea parties, and evening galas. A similar wardrobe was prepared for Lady Sarah, who wore a dramatic one-shoulder gown of deep blue silk to her daughter's debut. Arnold attended the festivities in the company of socialite Mitzi Newhouse and her son Si, who would take over the family's publishing business and became chairman of Condé Nast. Scaasi later remarked that while many of the English women appeared old-fashioned, wearing gowns of the 1930s and 1940s, what nonetheless gave them distinction was that they had brought out their most extraordinary jewels. As he wrote in his memoir *Women I Have Dressed (and Undressed!)*, "The hall was fairly sparkling with diamonds everywhere you looked."

Upon her return to New York, Russell continued her association with Scaasi, and went on to work for him and model in several of his fashion shows.

Towering above Serena, provocatively captured here by Cecil Beaton in Blenheim Palace for *Vogue* in August 1962, is the Carolus-Duran portrait of her great-great-grandmother Consuelo Vanderbilt, the ninth duchess of Marlborough. Surrounded by tapestries celebrating the first duke's victories, Serena confidently holds her own in her white guipure lace gown with a low-cut back.

Pictured outside Blenheim Palace with her grandfather, the tenth duke of Marlborough, the debutante wore this sporty blue-and-white ensemble to Gold Cup Day at Ascot. A version of what the designer called his "Parade suit," it was "formed and tailored with the perfection we see in menswear, but has all the molded curves, giving the waist-cinching jacket a most feminine look," the designer wrote in the *Philadelphia Inquirer* on May 14, 1962.

A *New York Herald Tribune* article in August 1962 featured sketches for Serena Russell's debut wardrobe, including the blue-and-white ensemble Beaton photographed for *Vogue* (previous page). The flounced dress shown at the right was designed so that the last tier could be removed to leave a shorter cocktail dress. The three sketches at the bottom of the page depict ensembles for the debutante's mother.

Selections from Scaasi's summer 1962 sketchbook (color, top) show variations of the floral dress and the flounced dress featured in the *Herald Tribune*.

Opposite: For Serena's mother, Lady Sarah Russell (née Churchill), Scaasi designed a version of his "Blackbird" dress using blue silk gros de Londres. Lady Sarah's husband, Edwin F. Russell, was at the time the publisher of *Vogue*.

Sketches by SCAASI

Debutante Serena Russell is headed for a fairy princess debut season. Daughter of Mr. and Mrs. Edwin Russell, granddaughter of the Duke of Marlborough and great-granddaughter of Mme. Jacques Balsan (Consuelo Vanderbilt) Miss Russell will make her bow to international society on July 14 at Blenheim Castle, the ancestral home of the Churchills who are Dukes of Marlborough. She will also be guest of honor at a ball given by Princess Margaret and will sit in the Royal Box at Ascot. Miss Russell is a recent graduate of Foxcroft. Her father is publisher of American Vogue.

Herald Tribune photo by JOE ENGELS

U. S. designer Scaasi has made her wardrobe for her coming out ball and debut festivities in England. Above: For Princess Margaret's ball she will wear candy pink triple flounced ballgown. The last flounce can be removed to leave a short dance dress. Top left: Wide collar frames bare shoulders . . . dance dress of Staron's blue cosmos silk print. Top right: For Gold Cup Day at Ascot, Scaasi designed white fitted silk and wool coat over pleated dress of navy and white dotted

Arnold Scaasi, American Couturier

During the 1960s, the high-end women's clothing industry underwent radical changes, as fashionable young women rejected the Parisian practices and styles of the postwar era. No longer interested in the dictates of the French couturiers, they began shopping in small boutiques, such as those that sprang up on the King's Road in London and in Greenwich Village in New York. The ready-to-wear industry followed suit, as women turned away from Parisian couture copies and toward the productions of young Seventh Avenue designers such as Geoffrey Beene, Oscar de la Renta, and Bill Blass. Although ready-to-wear came to dominate women's fashion in this period, Scaasi refused to head in that direction. He was fond of working directly with his high-society and celebrity clients; he had no interest in giving it up for the anonymous ready-to-wear industry. Moreover, while a high-end ready-to-wear dress could cost as much as a custom-made garment, the department store that sold it no longer took responsibility for making the necessary alterations to give it the proper fit. With the industry moving away from customer service, Arnold

This photograph of Scaasi's hostess ensemble from his first custom collection served as the frontispiece to a spread on home entertaining in the November 15, 1964, issue of *Vogue*. The model wears a pink crepe jumpsuit with a pistachio green satin housecoat.

The silk fabric with psychedelic stripes by the manufacturer Staron informed the design of these dinner pajamas, photographed on Veruschka in 1966 for *Vogue*. The photo, in which the model is posed provocatively with a Pop art sculpture by Marisol, perfectly conveys an aura of insouciant luxury and modernism, disguising what would be a relatively modest silhouette when standing. The designer used a similar wool fabric in a series of suits for clients such as Mitzi Gaynor and Barbra Streisand.

made the decision to stop his ready-to-wear line altogether and to create only custom clothing for private clients. As he put it, "My kind of customer, and you know I don't want everyone, is a woman who can first of all afford me, and who wants my taste."

In 1964, the first Scaasi couture collection was shown in Arnold's new salon at 26 East Fifty-sixth Street. As in the West Fifty-sixth Street town house and the Seventh Avenue showroom, the decor was by Valerian Rybar; the new salon featured mirrors, beige damask banquettes, and two enormous silver swans holding red roses. Attending the show were current and future clients Barbra Streisand, Joan Sutherland, Austine Hearst, and Brooke Astor. Arnold could now focus on what he loved best, dressing his ladies in luxurious clothing that suited their tastes, figures, and lifestyles. He paid attention to who

Some of Scaasi's most loyal clients were located in Palm Beach, Florida, including Therese Anderson, in the pink gown on the far right, and Mary Sanford, to her left. Every February, Arnold traveled to Florida to bring his collections to these clients.

In 1974, Scaasi purchased a summer home in the Hamptons. Built in 1910, it demanded extensive renovations — the designer incorporated the wrap-around porch into the living room, which opened it up for entertaining. Here, publishing executive Mary McNulty and Fernanda Wanamaker Gilligan both wear hand-painted crepe de chine caftans.

bought what, ensuring that no two women would turn up to the same function wearing the same gown — a growing problem caused by the expanding high-end ready-to-wear industry.

As Arnold's business developed, he further tailored it to match his clients' lifestyles. Many of his customers lived at least part of the year away from New York; rather than wait for his ladies to come to him, Arnold spent three to six months of the year traveling throughout the United States, showing his latest creations and taking orders. He often started in Palm Beach, where many of his clients wintered, and developed close relationships with social mavens such as Rose Kennedy and Mary Sanford. Often he would show his collection at charity events, eventually becoming as much a member of Palm Beach high society as his clients and, as of 1988, a homeowner there. From Palm Beach, he would travel to other affluent capitals, such as Dallas, Houston, Scottsdale, Los Angeles, San Francisco, Chicago, Philadelphia, Newport, Southampton, and Washington, D.C. Arnold's practice was to set up shop in a hotel suite and schedule appointments with his

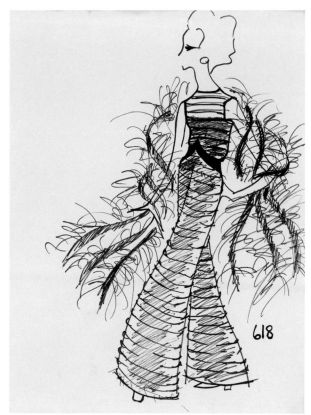

Above:
By the early 1960s, Scaasi began to use exotic and unusual materials that enthralled his clientele as well as magazine editors, who often chose his more outrageous designs to feature in fashion spreads. For his 1962 resort collection, he created pants made of python, dyed alligator, and guinea feathers.

Opposite:
This version of Scaasi's feather pants, in black marabou, was introduced in the fall 1974 collection and proved so popular that it was reintroduced in 1979. It epitomizes the designer's masterful use of varying textures while working in a single color palate. Tulle, silk satin, and feathers, in varying opacity, bring sophistication to this dramatic black pantsuit.

local clients and their friends, showing his designs, taking commissions, and making sure that women from the same cities didn't order the same dresses. The garments were then confected in New York, where clients would also come for their fittings. These fittings were done in three stages: the first visit was devoted to creating the basic slip and shaping the garment, the second to properly fashioning any pleats or tucking, and the third to fine-tuning details and marking the hem.

Arnold's work and travel habits mirrored his clients' lavish lifestyles, with social events in New York, weekends on Long Island, and frequent trips to Europe, the Caribbean, and Mexico. The same can be said of his designs and the materials he used: furs, feathers, rich embroideries, and beaded silks remained a staple of his collections and could be seen at the fanciest parties, society events, and ballrooms. Though most women were switching to ready-to-wear and the younger generation was turning its back on custom tailoring, Arnold persisted in creating luxurious fashions.

Central Park South

In 1962 Scaasi moved into a duplex apartment at 100 Central Park South. The 1930 building, designed by the architects Schwartz and Gross, did not boast an especially distinguished facade, but the interior layout was something else entirely. One entered Arnold's apartment on the eleventh floor, then descended from a loggia to a living room with twenty-five-foot ceilings and two-story windows overlooking Central Park. This dramatic space became the venue for lavish parties at which he entertained his celebrity and socialite clients, as well as the showroom where he often previewed his collections.

In January 1965, Arnold showed his spring collection in the comfort of his apartment on Central Park South. Fashion writers commented admiringly on the views over the park, which was covered in snow at the time. They were equally taken with the Bloody Marys their host served.

The two-story living room in Arnold's Central Park South apartment was dominated by a large baroque fireplace. The lavish apartment proved the perfect setting for this shot of an exuberant fishtail evening dress made of flowered organdy from Arnold's first custom collection in 1964.

The society pages frequently reported on Arnold's parties, establishing him as a fashionable figure in his own right. One of the earliest parties covered by the press was an after-concert affair for one of his newest clients, Australian coloratura soprano Joan Sutherland. When the diva performed at Carnegie Hall on February 18, 1963, she wore one of Scaasi's dramatic gowns with evening coat. Sutherland appeared onstage and opened her coat to reveal the dress and Scaasi's trademark matching coat lining, leaving the audience dazzled. The late-night party that followed featured a small dance floor — big enough for two couples — and a table laden with food.

Eventually the apartment served as the location for Scaasi's runway shows; his clients and the press were invited up and served Bloody Marys to keep them happy while they enjoyed the extraordinary views of the park. Even without a show, the press repeatedly featured Arnold's apartment, reporting on its interior design and describing the furnishings: a wolf rug in the living room; a Paul Jenkins abstract painting above the baroque fireplace; and, most of all, two ceramic chairs in the shape of hands designed by Pedro Friedeberg.

In 1983 the apartment was redesigned and Arnold asked his client and friend Louise Nevelson to contribute two sculptures: a white sculpture was inset into the ceiling in the entrance loggia, so that one could look up from the living room and see it, and a large black sculpture was placed above the fireplace. The apartment continued to be Arnold's space for entertaining, for exhibiting his growing and impressive art collection, and for showing his work. It served as a symbol of his success, both professional and social.

Known as "La Stupenda," legendary soprano Joan Sutherland became a client in 1964. Scaasi designed several gowns for her to wear during her concert performances and for traveling. The gown with the ruffled hem was called "Eve" from a series called "Garden of Eden." The designer recommended Sutherland wear bold designs, such as this, to play up her commanding figure rather than try to obscure it.

Arnold redecorated his Central Park South apartment in 1983 and asked his friend and client Louise Nevelson to create sculptures for the living room and second-floor loggia. She created a white ceiling for the loggia that reflected off the mirrors set into the walls.

Mrs. Joseph Norban's Wardrobe

To mark El Morocco's reopening on East Fifty-fourth Street in January 1961, the *New York Herald Tribune* shot Gillis McGill in this cocktail dress from Scaasi's spring 1961 collection in front of the club's trademark blue zebra banquettes.

Celebrities and socialites flocked to the posh nightclub El Morocco, including Doris Duke, Gloria Vanderbilt, Elizabeth Taylor, and Rita Hayworth, whose daughter Yasmin Agha Kahn would later become one of Scaasi's best clients.

Mrs. Norban would sometimes wear Scaasi's luxurious suits, such as this ensemble with a strapless pink satin bodice and skirt embroidered with wood and white glass beads, to El Morocco. Scaasi used the same fabric in a coat for Arlene Francis to wear on *What's My Line?*

During the 1960s, one of the most important events on many a fashionable New Yorker's calendar was the charity ball. As a social institution, the charity ball had replaced the lavish parties hosted by New York's most prominent families prior to 1913, when the 16th Amendment to the Constitution introduced income tax and personal wealth declined. As individuals stopped spending vast sums of money on such fêtes, charity balls proliferated during the first half of the twentieth century. Their organization fell to women who donated their time and energy to create grand receptions in the ballrooms of the Waldorf Astoria or the Plaza. The cream of New York society attended these events, with the proceeds going to causes such as the Red Cross and the Girl Scout Council of Greater New York.

Mrs. Joseph Norban, whose husband was a New York City real estate investor and part owner of the nightclub El Morocco, served on the organizing committee of the Lila Motley Cancer Foundation's Peacock Ball. The foundation had its origins in the Lila Motley League, a charity group created in 1945 by Lila Motley's friends following her premature death from cancer. Over the years, the foundation supported cancer research at New York University and established the Motley Radiation Therapy Clinic at the Hospital for Joint Diseases. The annual Peacock Ball, held on the first Saturday in May at the Plaza Hotel, was the height of the foundation's social season and a way to thank those who had been generous to the cause.

For the 1966 Peacock Ball, which she chaired, Mrs. Norban wore the Scaasi evening dress "Little Egypt" with its matching capelet. That year, Scaasi showed a number of evening dresses with raised hems and empire waists. "Little Egypt" was lavishly embroidered with coral and turquoise beads and silver tinsel in a stylized floral pattern, and lined with coordinating turquoise silk.

In 1966, the year Mrs. Norban chaired the Peacock Ball, the party had as its theme a "gala dinner on the Côte d'Azur." Needing a dress appropriate to the setting, she went to Scaasi, who made her a sumptuous beaded gown of turquoise and coral that he called "Little Egypt." The gown, with hem cut high in the front to bare the knees and trailing to the floor in the back, was embroidered with coral and turquoise beads and silver tinsel. Mrs. Norban also purchased several Scaasi ensembles over the years to wear to El Morocco or when traveling in Monte Carlo, which make evident her refined taste, as well as her love of beautiful clothing and craftsmanship.

Incorporating a color palate similar to "Little Egypt," this day suit in shades of coral and turquoise is a testament to Scaasi's dedication to opulent materials and workmanship. The bodice of the dress is built up from layers of turquoise chiffon, while the heavily beaded collar and cuffs act as trompe l'oeil necklace and bracelets.

Completely covered in small black silk bows, this daringly short trapeze dress of black tulle was worn by Mrs. Norban as well as Natalie Wood, who called it "the sexiest dress in the world." Wood wore the dress on an April 1966 episode of *What's My Line?*, in which Arlene Francis correctly guessed the star's identity.

In 1974, Scaasi incorporated innovative embroidered and appliquéd fabrics into his collection. This dress and matching white linen coat with faux capelet illustrate how the designer continued to produce his trademark ensembles, even as his silhouettes and hemlines changed with the times.

Barbra Streisand

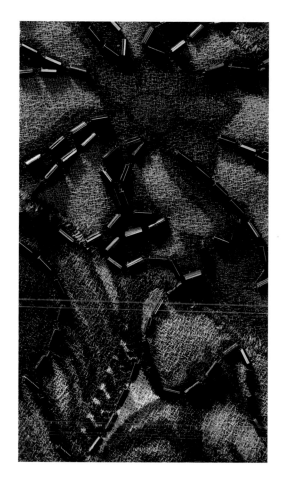

During the early 1960s, as Scaasi was rising to prominence in his profession, Barbra Streisand was gaining notice in the entertainment world. Arnold first started making Streisand's clothes in 1964, shortly after he began concentrating exclusively on custom work. The actress, known for her unique and very personal style, often wore vintage clothing — according to Arnold, she loved beautiful craftsmanship but couldn't find it in contemporary ready-to-wear. Streisand attended Scaasi's 1964 show wearing a fringed poncho and slouch hat, a hippie-style outfit that appalled the designer. But the twenty-two-year-old actress, having just opened in the Broadway musical *Funny Girl* and already well on her way to stardom, proved to be a loyal client for many years.

Perhaps the most famous ensemble Arnold created for Streisand was the black-sequined pantsuit he designed for the Academy Awards ceremony in 1969, when Streisand won an Oscar for her portrayal of Fanny Brice in the movie version of *Funny Girl.* Unexpectedly, when the stage lights hit the ensemble, the layers of black silk underlining and sequined tulle appeared transparent, and the star generated as much press for her "see-through" pantsuit as for her award.

Streisand continued to rely on Scaasi to create clothing both for her performances and for her private life. He designed a wardrobe for her European visit in 1966, and he created stunning evening ensembles from sari fabrics for her 1969 performances in Las Vegas.

Streisand was famous for her eclectic tastes in clothing, often wearing vintage pieces like many hippies of the time. Scaasi was able to give his high-profile client a luxurious version of hippie chic by pairing this dress with one of his favorite accessories, a piano shawl appliquéd with paisley fabric and embroidered with black beads.

Defying the custom of not wearing a competing designer's work to a fashion show, Streisand stands out at the 1966 Chanel show in Paris in a Scaasi leopard-printed calfskin suit with matching hat.

He designed the dresses she wore to the premieres of *Funny Girl* and *On a Clear Day You Can See Forever*, for which he also created the modern costumes Streisand wore in the film. In the 1968 best-dressed list, compiled from two thousand ballots sent to fashion editors, society editors, designers, columnists, and others in the fashion world, Streisand was named one of fashion's most imaginatively dressed women. She and Arnold created a "bohemian chic" look that suited the artist's age and personal style while maintaining the level of taste and refinement for which the designer was so well known.

In late 1968, Scaasi was commissioned to create the modern costumes for Streisand's third film, the Vincente Minnelli musical *On a Clear Day You Can See Forever.* "Having seen the costumes," *Women's Wear Daily* wrote on June 17, 1970, "one wag said the title of Barbra Streisand's new film should be 'On a Clear Day, You Can See Arnold Scaasi.'"

On a Clear Day marked the first time Streisand wore contemporary clothing on screen, her first two films having been period pieces. This remarkable suit, appliquéd with black vinyl, shows Scaasi at his most playful and experimental.

This wardrobe, designed for Streisand's 1970 visit to Montreal — she was seeing Prime Minister Pierre Trudeau at the time — incorporated fur into the accessories and as an embellishment. The bodice on this cream wool ensemble with matching hat and muff is embroidered with woven straw and rhinestones in a stylized floral motif.

Opposite:
Scaasi wanted to design a youthful ensemble for the twenty-three-year-old Streisand to wear to the 1969 Academy Awards. He updated this sequined pantsuit, previously created for Polly Bergen to wear in concert, with white collar and cuffs and satin bow at the front, which Streisand later called "kind of nutty."

Streisand accepted her Oscar for *Funny Girl* wearing what has become one of the event's most infamous ensembles. Scaasi's pantsuit of black sequined tulle lined with two layers of black silk chiffon appeared transparent when the glare from hundreds of flashbulbs hit it.

After the tumult the year before, Scaasi designed a more conservative ensemble for the actress to wear when presenting the Best Actor award (to John Wayne for *True Grit*) at the 1970 Academy Awards. Judiciously embroidered with Indian-inspired roundels, the pink crepe gown was topped off with a pillbox hat.

Fur

Scaasi's father, Samuel Isaacs, owned a fur-importing business in Montreal that specialized in fox pelts. He traveled throughout Canada visiting trappers and attending auctions in Prince Edward Island, Manitoba, and Nova Scotia; his wife and daughter both owned fur coats, jackets, and stoles. Arnold's familiarity with fur made him quite comfortable using it in his designs, along with other exotic pelts, such as alligator and snakeskin, and, of course, a multitude of various feathers. In 1958, he designed a collection of twenty furs for the Seventh Avenue furrier Ben Kahn. The show received rave reviews from the members of the press, who were struck by Scaasi's new cuts and uninhibited designs, such as a purple nutria greatcoat with large patch pockets, short free-swinging jacket made of tiger, and a twelve-foot boa of pastel badger.

Arnold continued to use fur in his fall collections, often lining or bordering his coats and jackets with it. A tweed coat lined in chinchilla from the fall 1961 collection often found its way into the press. In the late 1960s he designed a wardrobe for Barbra Streisand that featured evening jackets and coats liberally trimmed with fur, as well as matching fur hats and muffs (see pp. 96–97).

As luxurious clothing came back into fashion during the 1970s and early 1980s, Arnold's furs again caught the notice of fashion-conscious women. His 1970 collection for Ritter Brothers caused a "sensation" and was labeled "The Talk of the Town," while his 1976 collection for Ted Kahn was described as "Fur Out."

Scaasi's fall 1958 collection of furs for Ben Kahn garnered a large amount of press for the designer's unusual use of luxurious materials. His tiered Gold Crown chinchilla and satin bow cape was worn by Sophia Loren, who was then promoting her film *That Kind of Woman*.

Scaasi combined black fox and printed calfskin to resemble zebra in this stylish suit from later in his career.

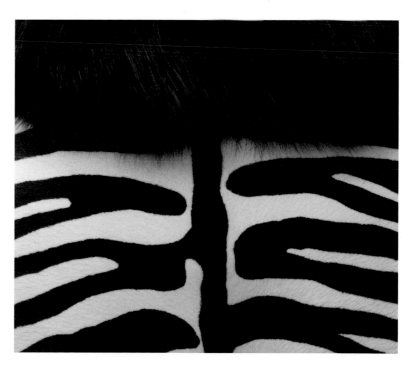

Right: Red fox collar and cuffs provide contrast to snow leopard in Scaasi's ski jacket for Ben Kahn.

By Evelyn Livingstone

FURRIERS have discovered a whole new animal world for fall. Zebras have been "fashion-broken," tigers tamed, snow leopards domesticated, hamsters, rabbits, and ponies rerouted from back yards to backs. This is the year, too, when favorites of yesteryear have

the return of with this wide d, full length

Scaasi's belted "Bengal tiger" coat with matching hat was drawn by the illustrator Margot for the *Chicago Daily Tribune* on July 27, 1959. The coat on the right is a ski jacket of snow leopard and red fox.

Although it may appear to be a long coat, this ensemble for Ritter Brothers actually consists of a short jacket and skirt of black broadtail trimmed with bands of silver fox. The coat to the right in this sketch is made of python trimmed with fox. "I like furs to give the feeling of luxury and quality," Scaasi noted in *Women's Wear Daily* on September 8, 1970.

Reminiscence: Diahann Carroll

Actress and singer Diahann Carroll is best known for her lead role in the television series *Julia*. With this pioneering role, she broke down stereotypes and was welcomed into the households of millions of Americans. For the stage, Scaasi designed classic, refined costumes for the singer, providing her with an alluring yet safe image.

"I hated going to fittings, but I enjoyed going to fittings with Arnold. He was a master, and I was fortunate that at a young age I recognized his talent and craftsmanship. I enjoyed watching him as he thought through a design and the garment came to life. When he worked with his assistants, he would show them how small alterations to a design could change the look of the garment.

"Often he and I would fall in love with a fabric. He brought them back from Europe, at times with a specific client in mind. We would discuss the fabric and how it could be used in a garment.

"Arnold's primary clientele were not performers, and I would often make suggestions about what might work better on the stage, such as changing the boning or using a stronger fabric. Two hours on stage is very hard on clothing — you need stronger fabrics. Arnold had a real sense of what to wear and when. On stage his expert tailoring and the beauty of his garments created a sensuality that was ladylike, never brash. His clothes were perfect for my Las Vegas concerts.

"Among the outfits Arnold designed for me, I particularly remember a navy blue and taupe tweed coat with a large fox collar lined with a beautiful blue silk. The coat was fitted at the waist, with inverted darts at the waistline giving flare to the skirt. It was extremely feminine. I've never had a better coat.

"When I visited President Kennedy, Arnold made me a beautiful white suit of heavy fabric — shantung, I think. It was elegant yet sensual. He designed the headband as well.

"I still have the black lace dress I wore in the 'Me and My Scaasi' ad. It's one I'll never be able to give up. Whenever I pull it out, it always surprises. It's so light and beautiful.

"And then there was the taupe and blue dress I wore for a performance at the Golden Globe Awards and afterward at a party honoring Aaron Spelling. I told Arnold I wanted something that would stand out because I wanted to impress Spelling and get a role on his series *Dynasty*. The colors of the dress were extraordinary — and I got the part."

— INTERVIEW BY PAMELA A. PARMAL, AUGUST 20, 2009

In May 1962 Carroll was invited to perform at the White House for President John F. Kennedy's forty-fifth birthday. She wore a white shantung silk suit from Scaasi's spring 1962 collection for the occasion; Carroll also wore the suit on a visit to London, accessorized with a pillbox hat. The suit was very popular and retailed for $695 at Henri Bendel.

Opposite: Carroll wore this chocolate brown and navy dress to the Golden Globe Awards in 1987. The dress is a revival of one of Arnold's most successful looks from his early career, which was featured in a 1954 ad in the General Motors "Body by Fisher" campaign.

Louise Nevelson

"Some people dismiss everything. At first clothing may have been a necessity, but sooner or later it grew like all creative things to the point where you can take material, like the paisley shawl I picked up in Maine for a few dollars, and tell Arnold Scaasi, 'If you put it on the outside and the chinchilla on the inside, I'll wear it.'"

— LOUISE NEVELSON, *WASHINGTON STAR*, OCTOBER 28, 1979

Louise Berliawsky Nevelson was born in Kiev, Russia, in 1899. At the age of six, she moved with her family to Rockland, Maine, where her father worked in a timber yard. Her early life in the Maine forests may have influenced her preference for working in wood, which became her most famous sculptural material. After her marriage to the wealthy ship owner Charles Nevelson, she moved to New York City. She later separated from her husband, spent several years studying art in Europe, then returned to the United States to make a home in Manhattan's Lower East Side. Much about Nevelson was larger than life: her monumental sculpture, her bohemian lifestyle, even her appearance. She was often seen wearing unexpected headgear such as jockey caps, babushkas, and Stetsons, along with three pairs of false eyelashes worn simultaneously.

During the 1950s and 1960s Nevelson gained increasing fame for her wooden sculptures. In 1967 the Whitney Museum of American Art organized a career retrospective, and PaceWildenstein, the gallery that represented Nevelson, set up an extensive lecture tour of college campuses. The gallery's director, Arne Glimcher,

"Darling, Miss America is cold," Scaasi recalls Nevelson telling him when commissioning this chinchilla-lined coat. The outside is made from an antique paisley shawl. Here Nevelson is shown with the playwright Edward Albee and his wife.

wanted to make sure that the artist appeared "pulled together" during the tour and arranged for her to meet Scaasi. When they first got together to discuss her wardrobe, Scaasi began by showing her low-key elegant black ensembles, to which Nevelson responded, "I'm just not a Scarsdale matron." Arnold was taken aback and after some thought replied, "You are certainly not a Scarsdale matron. You are the Empress of Art." And they set out to make her so.

From that day forward, Scaasi created extraordinary ensembles for Nevelson to wear for public appearances and openings as well as for work in her studio. Arnold and Nevelson selected luxurious sculptural fabrics, such as voided velvet and lamé, to create evening suits, dresses, and coats. The artist loved glamour and would often accompany Arnold to elegant parties at the Metropolitan Museum and elsewhere. For an opening of an exhibition of Nevelson's work in Berlin, he created a long black lace evening dress to be worn under a black dotted-net coat embroidered with polychrome sequins. The director of the museum claimed that Nevelson had brought glamour back to Berlin.

Nevelson's *Moving Waves and Tides* sculpture dominates the living room of Scaasi's Central Park South apartment in this shot for *Architectural Digest* from 1988. Scaasi stands flanked by his favorite Pedro Friedeberg hand chairs, with Mrs. Jonathan Farkas in the foreground.

Me and My Scaasi

As the American economy improved following the end of World War II and the Baby Boomers established themselves financially and socially, New York high society underwent a renaissance. By the late 1970s, the high life, which seemed to have been put on hold during the counterculture sixties and recession-wracked early seventies, returned full force, with charity balls, elaborate society weddings, and debutante coming-out parties. As these events flourished anew, so too did Scaasi's evening wear: the wives of newly wealthy New York entrepreneurs and financiers looked to Scaasi to ensure that they were appropriately dressed for each occasion. Scaasi's new clients included women such as Ivana and Blaine Trump, Gayfryd Steinberg, and Nina Griscom — "Les Nouvelles" of New York society.

Arnold's gala dresses showed up regularly at charity events, and pictures of the women who wore them often appeared in the press the next day. Ellin Saltzmann, a former executive of Saks Fifth Avenue, commented to Bernadine Morris of the *New York Times* that when she wore a dress by Scaasi more photographers were interested in taking her picture. As Arnold's clothing again became a regular feature, his name once again became

Never afraid of color, Scaasi boldly mixed saturated hues. The tri-color dress on the far left was produced in a variety of combinations, including pink, green, and white for Mary Tyler Moore to wear to the Golden Globe Awards in 1988.

With such devoted clients as Edna Morris, Arlene Francis, Austine Hearst, and Louise Nevelson, Scaasi underwent a complete renaissance in the 1980s. Younger clients, including Gayfryd Steinberg, Patty Davis Raynes, and Nina Griscom, also gravitated toward his opulent and colorful designs.

While young socialites wore his colorful and showy designs, *grandes dames* like Brooke Astor continued to look to Scaasi for refined and elegant pieces, such as this gray wool day dress.

prominent, and increasingly marketable, in the fashion world. In 1983, Saks Fifth Avenue began to offer his custom line in their stores, and the following year asked him to design a ready-to-wear collection: Scaasi's ready-to-wear business was reborn as Scaasi Boutique. Scaasi also began more high-profile licensing agreements, introducing wedding dresses, furs, handbags, sleepwear and lingerie, and even a fragrance.

In 1989, Barbara Bush chose a dress by Scaasi to wear to her husband's presidential inauguration. Scaasi's "Barbara blue" satin and velvet dress brought the designer even greater fame. He became a celebrity in his own right, alongside such select designers of the time as Gianni Versace and Giorgio Armani. Exhibitions at the New-York Historical Society in 1996 and the Fashion Institute of Technology in 2002 brought him still more recognition, as did the publication of the book *Scaasi: A Cut Above* (1996) and the memoir *Scaasi: Women I Have Dressed (and Undressed!)* (2004). With his insistence on creating luxurious custom clothing, so different from the trend followed by many late-twentieth-century designers, Scaasi holds an important place in the history of American fashion, carrying on the couture tradition that he inherited from his predecessors.

"There is a new society, and I love dressing them," Scaasi told *Women's Wear Daily* on January 19, 1989, and Gayfryd Steinberg was at its center. Called "Queen Gayfryd" by *W* in 1987, she is seen here in a Scaasi evening dress with her husband in their Park Avenue apartment.

Mrs. John A. Morris

Edna Morris epitomized the New York *grande dame*. Born on upper Fifth Avenue in 1908, she later attended Miss Porter's finishing school and then married John A. Morris, a New York stockbroker and former president of the Thoroughbred Racing Association. With her tall, elegant figure and inborn grace, she was a frequent figure at New York charity balls and society racing events, and her presence on the charities' ball committees ensured a successful and profitable gala.

Mrs. Morris was originally a client of Main Rousseau Bocher, better known as Mainbocher. The Paris-trained American designer had been dressing New York's most elegant and refined socialites since the late 1930s, when he relocated his business from Paris to New

From Scaasi's fall 1986 collection, this body-skimming gown is a rare example of Mrs. Morris's less colorful orders. It features a dramatic stand collar and cuffs trimmed with the same serrated fabric used for the shawl.

Mrs. Morris married into one of the oldest horse-racing families in America, whose stable color happened to be a shade of red adored by both client and designer. Scaasi created this long gown with a matching feather muff for her to wear to an awards ceremony in her honor at Belmont in November 1979.

On January 24, 1990, the Girl Scout Council of Greater New York hosted its annual winter gala at the Plaza as a tribute to Scaasi. Mrs. Morris (far left) was the general chairman, while Austine Hearst (center) and Gayfryd Steinberg (far right) also helped organize the black-tie event.

"Is her dress plugged in?" wondered *Women's Wear Daily* on January 28, 1988, after Mrs. Morris wore this pink gown with sparkling rhinestones to the annual Girl Scout Winter Festival in New York City.

York due to the impending war. When Mainbocher closed his New York salon in 1972, many of his clients, knowing that Scaasi was one of the few remaining designers in New York to make luxurious custom clothing, began to patronize the latter instead. According to Mrs. Morris, who was quoted in *Connoisseur* in 1984, "I always feel that when I go to a big dinner party in a Scaasi dress, I haven't overdone it or underdone it. You don't want your best dress to make you look like a circus dancer, but you still want to have that glamorous feeling, that it's the best you could do with the best you've got."

John and Edna Morris were frequent attendees at the debuts of Scaasi's custom collections; they would often hold hands and together decide which dress to buy Mrs. Morris for a birthday present. Much of her clothing was selected with events at the racetrack in mind. Summers in Saratoga required evening dresses for the many balls and parties held during the season, as well as suits and dresses for day wear. One such outfit, ordered in 1979 for the races at the Hippodrome de Longchamp outside of Paris, consisted of a fitted coat of grey fleece with sable cuffs and a striped wool dress to match.

The Fabrics

The lightweight printed silk poplin used for the "Moonflower Dahlia" from spring 1987 gives the dress more youthful buoyancy than his bubble-skirted dresses of the 1950s.

Throughout Scaasi's career, luxurious and extravagant textiles — with remarkable beading, pavéd crystals, embroidered raffia, hand painting, and passementerie — provided inspiration both for his designs and for the "story" behind each collection. At least twice a year he traveled to Europe to select fabrics from the leading manufacturers in Switzerland, France, and Italy, as reflected in a comment in *Women's Wear Daily* (June 9, 1961) that "every Scaasi collection is like a superb fabric documentary." During the 1970s, as most luxury brands went out of business, high-end fabric manufacturers saw a steep decline in demand and it became harder for Arnold to find fabrics that met his standards. But despite the difficulty, he always managed to locate extraordinary textiles that stood out from those used by other designers and showcased his love of color.

Arnold favored many of the laces, embroideries, and diamante textiles made by manufacturers such as Jakob Schlaepfer and Forster Willi, both located in Saint Gallen, Switzerland, which has been famous for its laces since the eighteenth century. Notably, Schlaepfer had developed a process for fusing rhinestones, pearls, and plastic paillettes onto cloth, making embellished fabrics lighter because metal fittings were no longer needed to set the stones. Arnold also prized the printed cloth made by the Italian firm Gandini, still a leading supplier to French haute couturiers and American designers.

From these high-end European textiles, Arnold created some of his most elaborate models, which in the 1980s found a ready audience among New York's most prominent socialites and his celebrity clientele. For his Scaasi Boutique line, he focused on less expensive though equally unique textiles, bought from suppliers with offices in New York, such as the Italian textile printer Ratti.

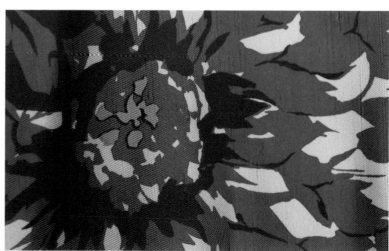

When Taylor's Passion perfume received the FiFi Award for most popular women's fragrance in 1988, the actress attended the ceremony in a gown of white organza embroidered with sprigs of violet that matched both the perfume bottle and her eyes.

Scaasi custom-designed this embroidery and had it manufactured in Saint Gallen, Switzerland, a town long famous for its embroidery industry.

Left and opposite: The Jakob Schlaepfer fabric used in this dress uses small metallic "stickers" fused directly to the silk to give it its shimmer. This allows the petals, which are all individually overcast, to remain stiff, giving the gown a feathery textural appearance. Gayfryd Steinberg wore the gown for a spread in *Manhattan* magazine in 1985. It was also ordered by Elizabeth Taylor.

Reminiscence: Joan Rivers

In the early 1980s, Rivers became the permanent guest host for the *Tonight Show with Johnny Carson*, and later launched her own late-night show on the Fox network. The comedienne was careful to choose Scaasi garments, such as this one, that would have visual impact above the interview desk.

"Arnold was and is as good as any of the great designers, like Yves Saint Laurent or Givenchy. I think he's very under-appreciated. His things were original. They were beautiful. The fabrics were magical. They were done individually — hand-sewn. Like him or not like him — and Arnold can be a pain in the butt — he's a true artist. His work is true couture. If he were in Paris, he would have had a totally different life. He should have been born French.

"When you had a piece made, you would go into this wonderful little salon, absolutely beautiful. The atmosphere! There were these two silver swans and I wanted them so desperately! First Arnold would show you dresses and then you'd look at fabrics and decide which ones to make the dresses with. It was very much a creative process. He'd always bring dresses out that were just scrumptious. You were never allowed to go into the sample room; he'd bring things out.

"I think Arnold knew drama, which I like. And I think he knew I loved showbiz, glamour. Theatrical, that's the way to put it. He totally understood how to design for the stage. I'm like a truck driver on stage — very rough on clothes — and Arnold's things were made very, very well. They didn't come apart. The way to tell a good dress is to turn it inside out and see what's happening, and Arnold's were beautifully done. The design process itself was semi-collaborative, but Arnold always won.

"I remember he did one dress for me that looked like something a girl with castanets would wear. It had a ruffled skirt and was all in beautiful black. When I'd go to parties, people would say, 'Where'd you get that? Who did that?' Arnold is amazing; he's got a great eye. He also made me a beautiful embroidered dress. We brought it out to California and I wore it on one of the red-carpet shows. I thought it was the most beautiful dress at the Academy Awards. I also wore it to Buckingham Palace.

"When you put on a Scaasi you felt like you had made it. It felt great and you felt great. I did a Revlon ad and I wore a red velvet Scaasi. I've remembered that dress for years. It was very tight fitting with a bell-shaped skirt. I tell you, Scarlet O'Hara, move over! It was so elegant, so beautiful."

— INTERVIEW BY PAMELA A. PARMAL, NOVEMBER 17, 2009

Scaasi designed many velvet gowns for Rivers, including this 1997 off-the-shoulder maroon version, which she described as "so Scarlet O'Hara."

Rivers wore this white spotted net dress from the spring 1982 collection, with the accompanying ruffled scarf, on the cover of *Los Angeles* magazine that November.

Me and my *Scaasi*

Reminiscence: Mary Tyler Moore

"I chose Arnold as my designer the moment I saw photos of his clothing. Like a child, I decided that I wanted to have that.

"Visiting Arnold was very entertaining. He would often arrive with sketches in hand of things he felt were appropriate, but he was also receptive to suggestions, especially about color. The first dress he made for me was a long gown that I wore to the 1988 Emmy Awards, when I was nominated for the best actress in a TV drama. The dress was made of lime green, pink, and white taffeta. Arnold asked me which colors I'd like and those are the colors I chose — I'm not sure why. He chose the jewelry, a large costume necklace with stones to match the colors in the dress. They were perfect together.

"I had a fairly tailored, conservative image from *The Dick Van Dyke Show* and *The Mary Tyler Moore Show.* Arnold recognized that and knew exactly how far to go. He never made anything too outrageous for me. He pushed me a step or two along the fashion runway, but always remained true to my character.

"Arnold designed evening and awards dresses, but he also did day wear for me. I remember a grey-and-white pinstripe suit that was worn with a frilly white blouse and fishnet stockings. You wouldn't think to put those things together, but Arnold did, and it worked. I also remember a navy blue lace short dress that I wore for the *Mary Tyler Moore* reunion show. It was lined with shocking green. His clothing was refreshing and always a surprise."

— INTERVIEW BY PAMELA A. PARMAL, AUGUST 25, 2009

Opposite.
Moore and Diahann Carroll were the only actresses among a slew of socialites in the "Me and My Scaasi" campaign, shot by Norman Parkinson, that debuted in the late 1980s.

Promoting her work in the miniseries *Lincoln,* Moore (shown on the left with husband Robert Levine) wore Scaasi's strapless tricolor gown of silk satin to the Golden Globe Awards on January 23, 1988. Scaasi also chose the necklace. On the right, Moore and Scaasi trip the light fantastic at the Girl Scout Council of America's 50th Anniversary dinner-dance in January 1990. The open bateau neckline was one of the designer's favorites throughout the decade.

Barbara Bush

Scaasi met Barbara Bush at a White House state dinner honoring the president of Iceland in 1986, just before her husband, then vice president of the United States, began intensely campaigning for the presidency. Arnold, not one to let an opportunity pass, "bumped into" Mrs. Bush after the dinner and offered his services as couturier. Two weeks later Mrs. Bush called him in New York, and he quickly became her favorite designer. As the two got to know each other better, they became good friends and together created a wardrobe that suited the future First Lady's personality, position, and taste. He designed most of the clothing she wore for the inauguration, including his now-famous "Barbara blue" evening dress with its deep sapphire blue velvet bodice and draped satin skirt. With the dress she wore her signature triple strand of pearls supplied by Kenneth Jay Lane.

Arnold recalls that Mrs. Bush loved pretty clothes. After the inauguration, she became an unexpected fashion figure. Newspapers reported on her design choices and heralded her down-to-earth nature and style. She chose to wear a Scaasi suit for an inauguration-week luncheon in her honor — a classic Scaasi design, with the blouse and the jacket lining in the same fabric. At one point during the luncheon, Mrs. Bush exposed the lining, like Arlene Francis and Joan Sutherland before her, and exclaimed in a self-deprecating tone, "Please notice — hairdo, makeup, designer dress . . . Look at me good this week. You may never see it again."

Scaasi redesigned his sapphire velvet and satin "side-draped polonaise short dress" from his fall 1988 Boutique collection for the new First Lady, lengthening the sleeves and hem and raising the bust line.

Both Brooke Astor and Austine Hearst had also purchased versions of the blue gown Bush wore to the inauguration. Scaasi called each personally to make sure they would not turn up at the ball wearing the same dress.

Old client meets new as Barbara and George Bush present Kitty Carlisle Hart with the National Medal of Arts on July 9, 1991. Both women are wearing Scaasi ensembles.

Because previous First Lady Nancy Reagan had favored red so heavily, Scaasi steered Bush away from the color. Her blue tweed suit with contrasting lining was one of many she ordered from Scaasi for daytime appearances.

Scaasi recalls the Bushes' daughter Doro saying that, of all the pieces the designer had made for her mother, this lavender wool coat was her favorite. Mrs. Bush wore it both to the church service after her husband was sworn in as president and, here, on the day the Bushes left the White House in January 1993.

Bush passed her love of Scaasi down to her daughter-in-law: Laura Bush attended the 2002 Kennedy Center Honors in a gown of black embroidered lace over fuchsia silk and Scaasi's fabric of choice for First Ladies, taffeta. Among the recipients that year was former Scaasi client Elizabeth Taylor.

Mrs. Bush continued to patronize Scaasi during and after her husband's presidency. When her daughter Doro married in a quiet ceremony in 1992, Arnold made the wedding dress of peach chiffon and lace. And when her son became president, daughter-in-law Laura in turn made the trip to the Scaasi salon in search of appropriate, stylish clothing, and Arnold began sewing for another First Lady.

Society Weddings

Known for his gala gowns, Scaasi was naturally often chosen to design dresses that marked important milestones in the lives of his clients and their daughters, such as bat mitzvahs, coming outs, and weddings. During the 1980s and 1990s, many of Arnold's clients brought their daughters to his salon for their special dresses. He designed exquisite wedding dresses for Patricia Jay Kluge, Patty Davis Raynes, Diahann Carroll, and Barbara Walters. His greatest press coverage, however, was owing to the dress he designed for the "wedding of the century" between Laura Steinberg and Jonathan Tisch, which united two of New York's wealthiest families.

Held in April 1988, the Tisch-Steinberg wedding epitomized the extravagant eighties, though the stock-market crash of the previous year and the declining economy made many wince at its excess. While the families tried to keep the financial details secret, some leaked out. It was reported that the total cost of the wedding

Feathers continued to play an important role in many Scaasi designs during the 1980s, including this wedding gown for retailer Eva Haynal Forsyth. The skirt is supported by many layers of stiff tulle, and the look could be balanced with an optional veil, also trimmed with ostrich feathers.

Scaasi began designing his first dedicated bridal collection in 1989 after the Steinberg-Tisch wedding. Initially sold exclusively through Saks Fifth Avenue, the line eventually expanded to retailers throughout the country.

Scaasi has been designing couture wedding gowns for a select clientele almost since he began. For the wedding of Shelley Davidson Susskind to Michael Dwayne Andreas in 1970, he fashioned a long-sleeved, high-necked gown of dotted Swiss organza with floral appliqués that complemented the yellow silk taffeta dresses with matching hats that he designed for the bride's attendants.

The 1988 wedding of Laura Steinberg and Jonathan Tisch was one of the most highly publicized social events of the decade. As well as the bride's gown, Scaasi also designed the bridesmaids' dresses, which were made of ivory moiré silk shot with gold.

reached $3 million, with the flowers alone estimated at $1 million and one of the two wedding cakes at $17,000. Five hundred guests were invited to the ceremony at Central Synagogue and the reception at the Metropolitan Museum, where a crew of seventy worked overnight to transform the great hall and restaurant into the replica of a late-eighteenth-century French palace.

The bride's stepmother, Gayfryd Steinberg, was a loyal Scaasi customer, and so it was to Arnold that Laura went for her dress and those of the attendants. The bridal gown of off-white taffeta was embroidered with silk and gold metallic thread and had a train seven feet long; a diamond-and-pearl tiara crowned the bride's head. The attendants wore off-white silk moiré shot through with gold.

That same year, Arnold launched a bridal collection for Eva Haynal Forsyth Enterprises, making Scaasi splendor available to brides throughout the country. In an article by Constance White for *Women's Wear Daily*, he stated, "It's a natural thing for me to do. I have always thought in terms of special occasions and the most special occasion in a young woman's life is her wedding."

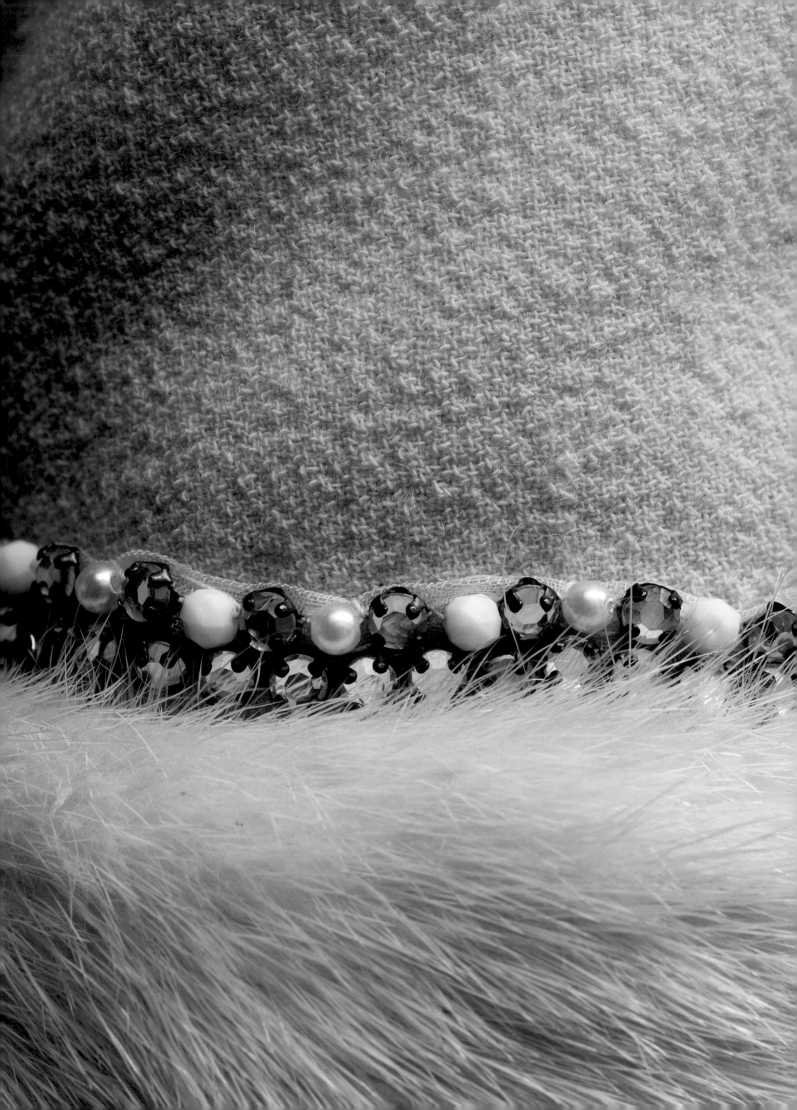

Chronology

1930 Arnold Isaacs born to Sam and Bessie Isaacs in Montreal, Canada (May 8)

1946–47 Travels to Australia with his sister Isobel and stays with his aunt Ida Wynn

1948–50 Returns to Montreal; studies at the Cotnoir-Capponi School of Fashion

1950 Studies at the Ecole de la Chambre Syndicale de la Couture Parisienne in Paris

Works for the house of Paquin for two months

1952 Travels to New York City, begins working as an assistant for Charles James

1954 Starts custom-design business out of his apartment at 140 East Fifty-eighth Street

Designs clothing for Mr. Fred and Lilly Daché runway shows and meets "It girl" and model Gillis McGill

"Body by Fisher" ad campaign; changes name to Scaasi

1955 Designs collection for Dressmaker Casuals (collection debuts May 19)

Meets Arlene Francis and designs clothes for her TV appearances on *What's My Line?* and *Home*

First *Vogue* cover (December)

1956 Shows first Scaasi ready-to-wear collection at the Plaza Hotel (May 28)

Meets Sophia Loren, who wears Scaasi clothes for *Vogue* spread

1957 Featured as one of "Six Top U.S. Designers" in *Look* (September)

Debuts collection at Sara Fredericks in Boston (December 5)

Hired to design wardrobe for *The Patrice Munsel Show* (December)

1958 Moves to 45 West Fifty-seventh Street, "a more sizeable establishment"

Begins to design jewelry with fall collection

Harper's Bazaar cover (March)

Designs fur collection for Ben Kahn (late summer)

Creates "Urban" collection of day wear for Townley Frocks (May)

Harper's Bazaar cover (September)

Designs costumes for Eva Gabor in *Present Laughter* (opened February 6)

Invited to the White House by Mamie Eisenhower and begins designing clothes for the First Lady

Designs costumes for Arlene Francis in *Once More, with Feeling* (September)

Wins Coty American Fashion Critics' Award or "Winnie" (October 1)

1959 Designs costume for Lauren Bacall in *Goodbye Charlie* (opened December 16)

Purchases Stanford White–designed town house at 26 West Fifty-sixth Street, off Fifth Avenue, with an interior designed by Valerian Rybar (June)

Wins Neiman Marcus "Distinguished Service to the Field" Award (September 14)

Arlene Francis wears Scaasi's fur chaps to guest-host *The Jack Parr Show* (July)

1960 Designs television, theater, and concert wardrobes for Polly Bergen, Hermione Gingold, and Rosemary Clooney

Name appears in the "On the Go" society column (October)

1961 Featured with other American designers in *New York Times Magazine* spread "Stars of the Evening" (January 22)

Closes town house on West Fifty-sixth Street and moves to larger showroom on the fourteenth floor of 550 Seventh Avenue (first show on June 12 at 5 p.m.)

Launches men's sweater collection for Vargeo and cravats for Hut Neckwear Co. (July)

Holiday magazine article on celebrities he has dressed, including Joan Crawford, Kitty Carlisle, and Dina Merrill (November)

Begins designing for Diahann Carroll

Associated Press story on lowered necklines highlighting Scaasi runs nationally (December)

1962 First show in Washington, D.C., for the March of Dimes held at Sheraton Park Hotel (January 18)

Dresses Cyd Charisse for *Family Weekly* (March 4)

Model Monique Chevalier wears Scaasi in TV ads for Coty lipstick (March)

Designs collection for girls aged seven to fourteen called "Little Women" for L. Wohl (debuts May 17)

Designs debut dress and wardrobe for Serena Russell Balfour and her mother, Lady Sarah Spencer Churchill (debuts July 13)

Sells town house on West Fifty-sixth Street and moves to 100 Central Park South (October)

First show on West Coast at Saks Beverly Hills (October 3)

Stops designing jewelry

Time reports that Scaasi's studio does $1 million in sales (December 21)

1963 Montreal manufacturer Glickman Dress manufactures forty-one models from spring collection for distribution in Canada (February)

Begins designing for Joan Sutherland (March)

Designs lower-priced line labeled "Scaasi Boutique for Martini" and produced by Sylvan Rich that continues even after he closes ready-to-wear business in April

Closes ready-to-wear business on Seventh Avenue (April)

Shows couture line at Sakowitz in Houston, Texas (September 9)

1964 Opens couture salon at 26 East Fifty-sixth Street (first show on April 20)

Begins designing clothes for Barbra Streisand

Designs nine-piece wardrobe for Geraldine Page in *P.S. I Love You* (opens November 19)

1965 Announces plans to open a Parisian couture house "in the next two years" (July 17)

Designs ten-piece wardrobe for Sharman Douglass to wear when hosting Princess Margaret and Lord Snowden on first trip to the U.S.; he will design her wedding gown in 1968 (November)

1966 Designs six ensembles for Streisand's European tour (February)

Lectures at the Royal Ontario Museum for Toronto Fashion Group, Inc. (February 9)

1967 Meets and begins designing for artist Louise Nevelson

First Palm Beach show of his collection at the Penthouse Suite of the Colony Hotel; meets Mary Sanford (February)

Mitzi Gaynor wears pink silk Scaasi ensemble to sing "Georgy Girl" at the Academy Awards (April 10)

1968 Designs contemporary costumes for Streisand in *On a Clear Day, You Can See Forever*

Designs twenty-five-piece collection for knitwear manufacturer Tannel (June)

Designs four ensembles for Streisand to wear to premieres of *Funny Girl* (September)

1969 Streisand wears black sequined Scaasi pant ensemble when accepting the Academy Award for her role in *Funny Girl* (April 14)

Designs costumes for Streisand's concert series in Las Vegas (June)

Designs handbag collection for Meyers Manufacturing Group (June); appears at Filene's in Boston to promote the line (November 24)

Purchases Cordelia Biddle Duke's home in the Hamptons (July)

Begins to design one collection a year instead of two; fall 1969 consists of 150 models, 50 more than usual

1970 Designs outfits for Streisand's visit to Canada (January)

Designs shoe collection for Battani and Taj Tajerie (January)

Designs second Academy Award outfit for Streisand, who presents Oscar to John Wayne for *True Grit* (April 7)

Introduces boutique ready-to-wear collection (September)

1971 Premieres spring collection at fundraiser for American Cancer Society at Four Winds, home of Patrick Lannan, in Palm Beach (February 5)

Dresses Palm Beach residents Therese Loy Anderson, Mary Sanford, Brownie McLean, and Ann Light for April-in-Paris Ball at Waldorf in New York City (October 29)

1972 Launches spring ready-to-wear collection for Paris-based Maria Moutet (April 14)

1973 Designs Diahann Carroll's peach crepe spiral-pleated dress for wedding to David Frost as well as trousseau (wedding cancelled in February)

Designs gowns for Ben Bagley's revue *The Decline and Fall of the Entire World as Seen through the Eyes of Cole Porter* (Chicago production, November)

1974 Designs hat collection for Dallas millinery company Bierner & Son (June)

Designs menswear for Henry Pollack

1975 "Fashion and Costume Retrospective — 1975" runway show celebrating twenty years of designs to benefit the New York City Opera and Ballet (November 6)

1976 Designs fur pieces for Ted Kahn (May)

Opens new salon on Fifth Avenue

1979 Accompanies Mrs. John Morris to Belmont (September 12)

1980 Offers his made-to-order collection at Saks Fifth Avenue, Houston and Beverly Hills

1981 "For Haute Couture, Just Spell Isaacs Backward" story in *People* (June 15)

"Hot Jazz" sequin ensemble used in ads for Clinique makeup (November)

1982 Joan Rivers appears on cover of *Los Angeles* magazine in white Scaasi gown (November)

1983 Begins selling custom collection through Saks Fifth Avenue

Joan Rivers appears on the cover of *People* in Scaasi ensemble (April 25)

1984 Diahann Carroll wears purple-and-brown Scaasi to Golden Globe Awards (Jan 28)

Scaasi Boutique ready-to-wear collection relaunched in fall (May 1)

"The Dramatist of Elegance" article in *Connoisseur* (July)

1986 Elizabeth Taylor wears black-and-white Scaasi evening dress to accept Lincoln Center film award (May 5)

Designs Barbara Walters's wedding dress for marriage to Merv Adelson (May 10)

Meets Barbara Bush

Designs costumes for Elizabeth Taylor's appearance on *The Bob Hope Show*

Begins designing for Joan Rivers's TV appearances

Thirty-seven Scaasi gowns worn to the opening of the Metropolitan Museum's Costume Institute exhibition "Dance, Dance, Dance" (December 8)

1987 Wins Fashion Council Designers of America award for his evening clothes (announced November, ceremony on January 11, 1988)

1988 "Me and My Scaasi" campaign debuts as first ad campaign to feature a couturier and his clients (March)

Designs wedding gown for Tisch-Steinberg wedding (April 18)

Elizabeth Taylor wears violet-covered Scaasi at Passion perfume launch (June 8)

Introduces bridal line for Eva Haynal Forsyth Enterprises (October)

Signs licensing agreement for intimate apparel and sleepwear

Designs fur line for Maximillian

1989 Barbara Bush wears custom blue gown to husband's inauguration (January 20)

Buys apartment at 1 Beekman Place

1990 Launches his first perfume scent, Scaasi (January)

Honored at the 50th anniversary Girl Scout Council of Greater New York gala (January 24)

Designs wedding gown for Kerry Kennedy to wear at wedding to Andrew Cuomo (June 9)

Designs fur collection for Mohl Furs

Creates "Cissy" doll in red gown for Madame Alexander

1991 Licensing agreement, Scaasi Dress to Depeche Mode Inc.

Licensing agreement for leather goods and handbags

Fur coat featured on cover of *Vogue* (August)

Dresses thirteen Miss America contestants (September)

Designs dress for Aretha Franklin's Radio City Music Hall concert (September 13)

1992 Designs plus-size line called "Scaasi X" (September)

1993 Licensing agreement, Warnaco's Designer Sleepwear (July)

1994 Begins selling dresses on the home-shopping network QVC

Closes boutique line

1996 Thirty-year retrospective, "Arnold Scaasi: The Joy of Dressing Up!", opens at the New-York Historical Society (September 30)

Scaasi: A Cut Above published by Rizzoli

Begins ready-to-wear collection, "Scaasi Nightlife" (December)

Wins American Council of Fashion Designers Lifetime Achievement award (November 14)

2001 Moves salon to 16 East Fifty-second Street

Designs wardrobe for Laura Bush's first European tour (May)

Purchases new home in Palm Beach (August)

"Scaasi: An American Icon" exhibition opens at Kent State University Museum, Ohio (June 29)

2002 "Scaasi: Exuberant Fashion — A Celebration of an American Couturier" exhibition opens at the Fashion Institute of Technology, New York City (October 15)

2004 *Women I Have Dressed (and Undressed!)* published by Scribner's

2006 "Arnold Scaasi: Master of Elegance" exhibition at Shippensburg University Museum, Pennsylvania

2008 Begins selling jewelry on HSN

"First Ladies and Fashion: Featuring the Work of Arnold Scaasi" exhibition at the Lincoln Museum, Indiana

2009 Acquisition of the Scaasi Collection and Archive by Museum of Fine Arts, Boston

2010 "Arnold Scaasi: American Couturier" exhibition and publication at the MFA (September 25)

List of Garments

All of the following garments were designed by Arnold Scaasi. Unless otherwise noted, all garments are courtesy:

Arnold Scaasi Collection—Gift of Arnold Scaasi
Made possible through the generous support of Jean S. and Frederic A. Sharf, anonymous donors, Penny and Jeff Vinik, Lynne and Mark Rickabaugh, Jane and Robert Burke, Carol Wall, Mrs. I. W. Colburn, Megan O'Block, Lorraine Bressler, and Daria Petrilli-Eckert

Page 18 Dress and coat ensemble (only coat shown)
Fall 1958
Patterned silk lamé, lined with silk plain weave
Coat center back: 107 cm (42⅛ in.)
2009.4065.2

Page 23 Dress and coat ensemble
Fall 1960
Patterned silk, lined with silk plain weave
Dress center back: 145 cm (57 1/16 in.)
Coat center back: 122 cm (48 1/16 in.)
2009.4011.1–2

Page 24 Dress and stole ensemble
Fall 1982
Silk plain weave taffeta dress with tulle and synthetic horsehair infrastructure; silk plain weave taffeta stole
Dress center back: 147 cm (57⅞ in.)
Stole: 286 x 88 cm (112⅝ x 34⅝ in.)
2009.4030.1–2

Page 28 Dress and coat ensemble (only dress shown)
Fall 1958
Silk satin lined with silk plain weave
Dress center back: 118 cm (46 7/16 in.)
2009.4116.2

Page 32 Dress and coat ensemble
1958
Silk satin coat lined with silk and silver metallic matelassé; silver metallic matelassé dress with applied girandole brooch and silk satin ribbon
Dress center back: 136 cm (53 9/16 in.)
Coat center back: 154 cm (60⅝ in.)
2009.4013.1–2

Page 40 Dress and coat ensemble (only dress shown)
1958
Printed silk plain weave with tulle infrastructure, silk satin bow
Dress center back: 88 cm (34⅝ in.)
2009.4035.1

Page 57 Dress and coat ensemble (only dress shown)
Fall 1959
Silk chiné plain weave taffeta with tulle underskirt
Dress center back: 87.6 cm (34½ in.)
2009.4064.1

Page 78 Feather trouser ensemble with scarf
Fall 1974 or 1979
Silk satin pants trimmed with marabou feathers; tulle blouse trimmed with silk ribbon; silk plain weave bustier; tulle shawl trimmed marabou feathers
Blouse center back: 57 cm (22 7/16 in.)
Trousers center back: 113 cm (44½ in.)
Scarf: 180 x 65 cm (70⅞ x 25 9/16 in.)
2009.4031.1–3

Page 84 Dress and jacket
1960s
Dress skirt and jacket of silk twill embroidered with plastic, glass, and silk cord; silk satin bustier
Dress center back: 66 cm (26 in.)
Jacket center back: 55.5 cm (21⅞ in.)
2009.4062.1–2

Page 87 "Little Egypt" dress and capelet (only dress shown)
Spring 1967
Silk plain weave dress and jacket embroidered with plastic, coral, glass, and metallic foil, lined with silk plain weave taffeta
Dress center back: 113 cm (44½ in.)
2009.4059.1

Page 89 Dress and jacket
Spring 1968
Silk plain weave dress and jacket embroidered with coral, plastic, glass, and silk plain weave chiffon; jacket lined in silk plain weave
Dress center back: 92.7 cm (36½ in.)
Jacket center back: 41.3 cm (16¼ in.)
2009.4060.1–2

Page 90 Dress
Spring 1966
Cotton plain weave dress; overdress of tulle with applied silk bows
Center back: 90 cm (35 7/16 in.)
2009.4057

Page 91 Dress and coat ensemble
Spring 1977
Linen plain weave coat lined with silk plain weave, embroidered and appliquéd; dress of silk plain weave, embroidered and appliquéd
Dress center back: 80 cm (31½ in.)
Coat center back: 104.1 cm (41 in.)
2009.4061.1–2

Page 92 Dress and shawl ensemble
1970
Printed wool plain weave crepe embroidered with
glass beads; silk plain weave shawl appliquéd
with wool crepe and beaded, silk fringe
Dress center back: 130.8 cm (51½ in.)
Shawl: 164 x 121 cm (64 9⁄16 x 47 5⁄8 in.)
2009.4020.1–2

Page 94 Motorcycle suit designed for *On a Clear Day,*
You Can See Forever
1969
Printed wool twill appliquéd with vinyl
Cape center back: 64.1 cm (25¼ in.)
Trousers length at side seam: 104.1 cm (41 in.)
Cap length: 30 cm (11 13⁄16 in.)
2009.4088.1–3

Page 97 Fur ensemble
1971
Wool plain weave crepe bolero lined with silk satin
and trimmed with mink; wool plain weave crepe and
silk dress embroidered with raffia and rhinestones,
lined with silk; matching fur hat and muff, lined
with silk satin
Jacket center back: 42 cm (16 9⁄16 in.)
Dress center back: 144 cm (56 11⁄16 in.)
Hat: 13 x 20 x 21 cm (5⅛ x 7⅞ x 8¼ in.)
Muff: 22 x 27 cm (8 11⁄16 x 10 5⁄8 in.)
2009.4083.1–4

Page 99 Tunic and trouser ensemble
1969
Silk tulle embroidered with sequins, cotton collar and
cuffs, silk satin bow, lined with silk plain weave
Tunic center back: 66 cm (26 in.)
Trousers center back: 108 cm (42½ in.)
2009.4085.1–2

Page 100 Three-piece suit (blouse not shown)
1970s
Printed calfskin trimmed with fox fur
Jacket center back: 74 cm (29⅛ in.)
Skirt center back: 50 cm (19 11⁄16 in.)
2009.4091.1–2

Page 103 Two-piece suit
1970
Broadtail trimmed with fox fur, lined with silk
plain weave
Jacket center back: 58 cm (22 13⁄16 in.)
Skirt center back: 83 cm (32 11⁄16 in.)
Frederick Brown Fund
2010.24.1–2

Page 108 Woman's coat
1972
Wool twill tapestry, lined and trimmed with
chinchilla fur
Center back: 136 cm (53 9⁄16 in.)
2009.4047

Page 114 Dress
Fall 1987
Silk plain weave taffeta
Center back: 132.1 cm (52 in.)
Center front: 125.7 cm (49½ in.)
2009.4108

Page 118 Dress and stole ensemble
Fall 1986
Tulle appliquéd with silk damask, silk plain weave
bodice, tulle underskirt
Dress center back: 173 cm (68⅛ in.)
Stole: 198 x 78 cm (77 15⁄16 x 30 11⁄16 in.)
2009.4019.1–2

Page 121 Dress
Fall 1987
Tulle with fused rhinestones, silk plain weave
underdress
Center back: 158 cm (62 3⁄16 in.)
2009.4046

Page 122 "Moonflower Dahlia" dress
Spring 1987
Printed silk twill lined with silk plain weave,
tulle infrastructure
Center back: 147 cm (57⅞ in.)
2009.4012

Page 125 Dress and shawl ensemble (only dress shown)
Spring/Summer 1986
Silk plain weave appliquéd with silk plain weave
petals with fused synthetic paillettes, tulle underskirt
Dress center back: 132.1 cm (52 in.)
Shawl: 154 x 50.8 cm (60 5⁄8 x 20 in.)
Gift of Gayfryd Steinberg

Page 128 Dress and capelet ensemble (only dress shown)
Spring 1982
Flocked synthetic tulle with horsehair braid, silk tulle
and synthetic plain weave underdress
Dress center back: 137 cm (53 15⁄16 in.)
2009.4024.1–2

Page 132 Dress
Fall 1988
Silk satin and silk velvet lined with silk plain weave
Center back: 137 cm (53 15⁄16 in.)
2009.4026

Page 136 Wedding dress and veil (only dress shown)
1989
Silk satin with ostrich feathers, synthetic tulle
underskirt
Dress center back: 185 cm (72 13⁄16 in.)
2009.4053.1

Photo Credits

15: Richard Rutledge/*Vogue*, © Condé Nast Publications

19 (top), 49: As Seen in U.S. *Harper's Bazaar*

26 (top): © Condé Nast Archive/CORBIS

27 (top), 52, 85 (bottom), 98 (bottom): © Bettmann/CORBIS

27 (bottom): Brooklyn Museum Costume Collection at The Metropolitan Museum of Art, Gift of the Brooklyn Museum, 2009, Gift of Mrs. John de Menil (2009.300.816). Image © The Metropolitan Museum of Art.

33 (top): © Playbill. Used by permission.

34 (left): Alfred Eisenstaedt/Time & Life Pictures/Getty Images

35 (bottom): CBS/Landov

36: John Rawlings/*Vogue*, © Condé Nast Publications

46 (bottom left and bottom right): © 2010 Artists Rights Society (ARS), New York / VG Bild-Kunst, Bonn

48: Walter Sanders/Time & Life Pictures/Getty Images

51 (bottom): © 2010 The Andy Warhol Foundation for the Visual Arts, Inc. / Artists Rights Society (ARS), New York

55: Ed Clark/Time & Life Pictures/Getty Images

56 (left), 58 (top): Image by National Park Service and the U.S. Navy, courtesy the Dwight D. Eisenhower Library

61, 62, 66 (top right), 67 (left): Ronny Jaques/trunkarchive.com

66 (top left): *Camille* © Turner Entertainment Co. A Warner Bros. Entertainment Company. All Rights Reserved.

66 (bottom): Bruce Davidson/Magnum Photos

68, 69: Cecil Beaton/*Vogue*, © Condé Nast Publications

71: © Melvin Sokolsky

74, 79 (left): Horst P. Horst/*Vogue*, © Condé Nast Publications

75: Image © Condé Nast Archive/ CORBIS; artwork © Marisol Escobar/ VAGA, New York

77: © Elaine M. Salkaln

81 (left): Ruth Orkin/Getty Images

82 (left): Bob Gomel/Time & Life Pictures/Getty Images

90 (left): © Stephen Schapiro

93 (bottom): Bill Eppridge/Time & Life Pictures/Getty Images

95 (top left): © JP Laffont/Sygma/ CORBIS

98 (top): AP Photo/George Birch

102 (bottom): Unknown artist/*Vogue*, © Condé Nast Publications

104: © 1978 John Engstead / mptvimages.com

106 (top): Cecil Stoughton, White House/John F. Kennedy Library, Boston

106 (bottom): Keystone/Hulton Archive/ Getty Images

107: Ron Galella/WireImage/ Getty Images

109: AP Photo/Brocklet

117: Arnold Newman/Getty Images

120 (top): © Anthony Edgeworth

124 (top left), 131 (left): Time Life Pictures/DMI/Time & Life Pictures/ Getty Images

125: Courtesy Arnold Scaasi

127: © Douglas Kirkland/CORBIS

129 (right): Dave Allocca/DMI/ Time & Life Pictures/Getty Images

130: © Norman Parkinson

131 (right): Robin Platzer/Twin Images/ Time & Life Pictures/Getty Images

133 (bottom), 134 (top and bottom), 135 (top): George Bush Presidential Library and Museum

135 (bottom): Eric Draper/White House/ Getty Images

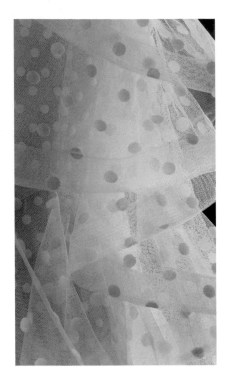

MFA Publications
Museum of Fine Arts, Boston
465 Huntington Avenue
Boston, Massachusetts 02115
www.mfa.org/publications

This book was published in conjunction with the exhibition "Scaasi: American Couturier," organized by the Museum of Fine Arts, Boston, from September 26, 2010, to June 19, 2011.

The exhibition is made possible by the David and Roberta Logie Fund for Textile and Fashion Arts and the Loring Textile Gallery Exhibition Fund.

Generous support for this publication was provided by the Ann and John Clarkeson Lecture and Publication Fund for Textiles and Costumes.

ISBN 978-0-87846-758-7 (hardcover)
ISBN 978-0-87846-759-4 (softcover)

Library of Congress Control Number: 2010925902

The Museum of Fine Arts, Boston, is a nonprofit institution devoted to the promotion and appreciation of the creative arts. The Museum endeavors to respect the copyrights of all authors and creators in a manner consistent with its nonprofit educational mission. If you feel any material has been included in this publication improperly, please contact the Department of Rights and Licensing at 617 267 9300, or by mail at the above address.

While the objects in this publication necessarily represent only a small portion of the MFA's holdings, the Museum is proud to be a leader within the American museum community in sharing the objects in its collection via its Web site. Currently, information about more than 330,000 objects is available to the public worldwide. To learn more about the MFA's collections, including provenance, publication, and exhibition history, kindly visit www.mfa.org/collections.

For a complete listing of MFA publications, please contact the publisher at the above address, or call 617 369 3438.

Front cover: Detail of dress, fall 1988, silk satin and silk velvet lined with silk plain weave (see p. 132)

Back cover: Detail of three-piece suit, 1970s, printed calfskin trimmed with fox fur (see p. 100)

All garments in this book were photographed by Michael Gould of the Imaging Studios, Museum of Fine Arts, Boston, except where otherwise noted.

Copyedited by Jodi M. Simpson
Designed by Susan Marsh
Typeset in Gotham by Duke & Company
Produced by Terry McAweeney
Printed and bound at CS Graphics
PTE LTD, Singapore
Printed on 150 gsm Enova Matt

Available through D.A.P. /
Distributed Art Publishers
155 Sixth Avenue, 2nd floor
New York, New York 10013
Tel.: 212 627 1999 · Fax: 212 627 9484

FIRST EDITION

Printed and bound in Singapore
This book was printed on
acid-free paper.